PARADISE

PARADISE

MEMORIES OF HILTON HEAD IN THE EARLY DAYS

Nelle and Ora Smith

FULL-SERVICE   BOOK-MAKERS

ESTD.   1999

With grateful acknowledgment to the Hilton Head Chamber of Commerce for permission to utilize material from their past brochures.

"Giving Fraser His Due" and "A return to Manners" published with permission from the Hilton Head *Island Packet*.

PUBLISHED BY
The Chapel Hill Press, Inc., Chapel Hill, NC

ISBN 978-1-59715-175-7
Library of Congress Catalog Number 2018930586

First Printing
Printed in the United States of America

PUBLISHER'S CATALOGING-IN-PUBLICATION DATA
(Prepared by The Donohue Group, Inc.)

Names: Smith, Nelle. | Smith, Ora Elliott.
Title: Paradise : memories of Hilton Head in the early days / Nelle and Ora Smith.
Description: Chapel Hill, NC : The Chapel Hill Press, Inc., [2018]
Identifiers: ISBN 9781597151757
Subjects: LCSH: Hilton Head Island (S.C.)—History. | Tourism—South Carolina—Hilton Head Island—History. | Hosting of sporting events—South Carolina—Hilton Head Island—History. | Smith family—South Carolina—Hilton Head Island—History.
Classification: LCC F277.B3 S658 2018 | DDC 975.799—dc23

DEDICATION

First of all, I want to dedicate this book to my family: my husband John, Gettys, Spencer, Ora Elliott, Ellen, Christine, Cotter, and Samantha Smith, and my sister, Isabel Yates. I also want to honor Katherine Tandy Brown, my excellent memoir teacher who first encouraged me to write; Toni Valley Johnston, who transcribed all of John Gettys Smith's dictated tapes; and my typist, Cindy Carrigan, who could read my writing and my mind as well.

I want to thank my publisher, Edwina Woodbury, who immediately said that this is a story that needs to be told. Her calm, reassuring manner and constant support provided a smooth transition from our project to this book.

I also want to thank all of the people who have touched and enriched our lives during our years on this Island. So many of my good friends who contributed to the fabric of our lives are not even mentioned, but I hope they know their value to the Smith family and to the Island. Without them, and all the unsung heroes, there would be no book.

Contents

Foreword

Sharing Our Island Memories

Living on Hilton Head Island in the early 1960s and 1970s was a remarkable experience. Was it Paradise ... or Camelot ... or Utopia ... or ... "The Days of Wine and Roses"? It was all of those things. In 1963, my husband, John, began a journal—his memoirs writing a history of this idyllic place. He realized the importance of preserving the history of the beginnings of this new community.

Years later, after his debilitating stroke, I promised him that I would finish his memoirs and write my own, too. The Island's history must be told, and our family was blessed to have lived it.

How did the Island evolve into the metropolis it is today? Before I can tell my memories of the "firsts" of so many happenings, I want you to close your eyes, use your imagination, take deep breaths, and think peaceful thoughts. It was a quiet, simpler time with almost all dirt roads, no traffic, and definitely no traffic lights. Everyone wants to know what it was like *then*, and I can't wait to tell you.

Paradise

"It's paradise!" John screamed enthusiastically to me in the spring of 1963. He had just returned after an interview with Charles Fraser for the public relations job at Sea Pines. John added, "And, if I get the job, we're moving! It's the chance of a lifetime!"

I was upstairs getting our little ones bathed and ready for bed, and I was so happy for him, but also worried. The chance of his really getting the job were *slim*. After all, he had no work experience in marketing or public relations; he had double majored in college in history and art. Since then, he had taught school, worked for the Rock Hill newspaper—covered the sports, taken all the photos, and written the copy—and worked tirelessly as a volunteer to try to save historical homes and places. This had begun in the late 1950s when preservation was not popular. Progress was considered as "tear down" the old homes that need repairing and put up something new in their place, even if it was ugly or ruined the beauty of the area. This was before Jackie Kennedy restored the White House.

York, South Carolina, was threatened with the teardown of an antebellum home in a historic, beautiful neighborhood—to be replaced by a Winn-Dixie supermarket. John immediately began organizing many volunteers who wanted to preserve the area. He founded a museum, promoted tours of historic homes with great success, and opened a restaurant on the weekends with a friend at the Brickhouse in Brattonsville, which was one of four falling-down houses. This was long before this area was included on the National Historic Register. There had been no previous work done on this historic home, so they literally cleaned it out and painted from top to bottom. John was considered by many as the "village idiot," as he also began painting an old store downtown by himself in his spare time.

He had the vision to see how architecturally beautiful the stores were and submitted sketches that were put on display in the window of Belk's Department Store. The fight went on for years between those who valued history and beauty, and those who considered those ideas old-fashioned and antiprogress. Their slogans were "Don't fix it up." "Just bulldoze it down." "Think modern, new."

I was very much involved with all this, too, as wives are. To save money on the museum, all the artifacts were moved to our house, which we were restoring. At a moment's notice when the doorbell would ring, I would become a docent as well as a mother. I'd alert our little boys, scoop up our baby girl, and welcome the visitors, hoping they'd leave a sizeable donation. I'd give the tour inside the cases of memorabilia. The children learned if they were good to expect a treat afterward. We lost the fight to save that house, but John had put York in the news with all the publications and photos. The newspapers drew hundreds to the tours of its historic homes.

Would these efforts help him get a job in public relations? I was afraid not, but I agreed that we should move somewhere that cared about its environment and that valued beauty, even though it would be very painful for John to leave his family, cousins, and friends. For generations his ancestors had been in this county. After putting together a scrapbook showing what he had done, John began apply-ing for jobs in the few places that cared about the environment.

When we saw in the *State* newspaper that David Pearson was leaving his public relations job at Sea Pines to join the Peace Corps, I urged John to apply. Now, I was *concerned* that he might not get this job.

John's First Interview with Charles Fraser

After the most attractive receptionist, Lou Dykes, welcomed me and indicated that Charles was ready to see me, I arose and went to the door, needless to say filled with some fear and trepidation. Getting away from York, the old hometown that I had a passionate love-hate relationship with, was absolutely vital to me.

The job on this wild, virtually uninhabited, semitropical island in South Carolina seemed to offer a strange escape paradise. I had no idea what the job of public relations–marketing for the Sea Pines Company really involved, but I honestly had no real fear that I could not do whatever it was.

Meeting Charles for the first time was quite an experience. I am six feet tall and, at the time in the summer of 1963, still weighed precisely what I weighed when I was in college—170 pounds. I was lean to the point of thin and brunette as my mother's family generally is. Charles, in contrast, was a short, somewhat boyish-looking man with blue eyes and curly brownish hair. His face was round and full. His eyes were intent, extremely intelligent, and clear.

This was the first serious interview I had ever been subjected to in the office of a potential employer. Charles wasted or spent very little time on the normal Southern pleasantries, despite the fact that he was a native of a tiny backcountry crossroads' town of Hinesville in southern Georgia. Due to my attempts to make a good impression on him, I can remember almost nothing about that initial interview except his asking me what magazines I read. From the way he asked, he obviously considered my answer to be important to the outcome of the interview. It was not exactly a question I had anticipated. I was prepared to recite all of the trials and tribulations of my early work in historic preservation and historic zoning in York. The only thing that came to my mind in response to the question about magazines I read was to blurt out something about *Time* and *LIFE* magazines. With a Machiavellian sort of smile, Charles responded, "Surely, you read something better than that."

I think I answered, "I read a lot of books, biographies, histories, novels, and I also read *American Heritage* and *Horizon* magazines, either the ones that I can subscribe to or the ones that my father-in-law subscribes to." That prompted a much more genuine interest in my intellect and the prospects of my being a part of his Sea Pines Company.

His Sea Pines Company, I was soon to learn, was rather minuscule. Its core staff of executives and secretaries were housed in the two small, cubistic framed buildings joined together by an open breezeway. The receptionist/secretary's area occupied the majority of the front building, and the doors led off of this space on one side to Charles's office, a rather small space, and on the other side to a much smaller space for the company treasurer. That should have given me an early indication—which it did not—of Charles's appreciation for the financial stability of his would-be pioneering company. The treasurer's office comprised nothing more than space for a small desk and a chair for a visiting supplicant. Charles's office was tastefully furnished in spare modern Scandinavian style, as was the general feeling of the office complex itself.

Our interview in the office was rather brief. Charles was dressed as if he might be on an African safari rather than a South Carolina sea island: khakis and a safari-type shirt with multiple pockets and boots, which turned out to be snake boots. The introduction to the snake-bite-prevention foot gear was invariably accompanied with the additional information that the boots were recommended by the late doctor, whomever he was, a professional in the world of snakes. Apparently, the marketing department of the boot company found no irony in using the slogan that the boots were recommended by the late doctor and assumed all readers would surmise the doctor died quietly at home in bed of old age rather than, as was implied, by a deadly venomous bite.

Charles rose from the desk, indicating the formal part of our interview in his office was complete, and said, "I will now show you Sea Pines Plantation." I had absolutely no idea of what to expect on this grand tour. What I was introduced to, over the next half hour or so, was an exquisitely beautiful semitropical wilderness, bordered by the Atlantic Ocean and marshes, inhabited by exotic birds and other wildlife. All along the ocean and on the interior, giant pines reached toward the sky. Along the beach, they were lined like sculptured sentinels reminiscent of Japanese paintings. Beneath was an understory of dense yaupon, scrub Palmetto, bay hardwoods and native waxy dark-green-leaved Magnolia grandiflora. All manner of semitropical foliage flourished. The forest, both high and low, was studded by magnificent Palmetto trees—the sable palm, South Carolina's official state tree, whose trunks had helped the native patriots during the first decisive battle of the American Revolution at Fort Moultrie off Charleston.

The Second Interview

John didn't hear back from Charles for two or three weeks, so he called, hoping that he had not left any stone unturned, saying he was still *so* interested, asking if he needed more information, and so on. After that call, I think Charles called Fitz McAden, who was head of the state's Parks and Tourism Organization in Columbia, asking him what he thought about John Gettys Smith, who had applied for the public relations job at Sea Pines. Thankfully, Fitz answered very positively. "He has done wonders with the publicity for York, strictly as a volunteer and never gives up. I think he'd work like a dog!" Fitz stated that he thought John was very talented at marketing even though he had no training. "He's very creative, enthusiastic, and has vision."

This led to John's second interview in a phone call from Charles, and he added, "Why don't you bring your wife and maybe stay a few days?" We were so *excited*! I called my girlfriends and borrowed their best clothes so that I could *last* for five days, if *needed*, looking good!

John kept saying to me, "Listen carefully, Nelle. Don't talk too much [which I am prone to do]. Memorize the names. You're really good at that. And I'll concentrate on answering the questions." We were both more than a little nervous.

Nelle's First Time Meeting Charles and His Staff

I remember well this first time I met with Charles Fraser; Charles Norvell, manager of the William Hilton Inn; Charles Doughtie, owner of the Island Shop, the only gift shop adjacent to the William Hilton Inn; Charles James, treasurer of Sea Pines Co.; Mary Stone, a young, attractive social director, who later married Charles Fraser; and Mary Dunn, the only secretary for the entire Sea Pines office. I remember thinking I was losing my mind, as John and I were being interviewed for that job in the summer of 1963. Everyone in the small group was named either *Charles* or *Mary*. Was I crazy or just not listening?

Since this was the first time that I had been asked to come for an interview along with John, I expected there would be some Southern pleasantries and questions to me about our children, but nothing doing. Business began as soon as lunch was served.

As John took his first bite of a hamburger, Charles began by asking rather mischievously with his eyes twinkling, "And now, John Gettys Smith [I can visualize him right now], if I choose *you* to be my public relations director, how would you *begin* to attract *people* to *buy property* on this Island?" I felt utter panic and nearly choked for John. I could see that Charles was no ordinary man, that he wanted a real answer. This was no idle question.

Fortunately, John chewed very slowly, breathed deeply, I'm sure, and accepted the challenge. I've long forgotten John's answer, but he seemed to love the competition of ideas and got along famously with Charles.

I, of course, was enchanted with the Island and prayed that John would get the job!

Getting the Job

John and I were on pins and needles back in York, hoping to hear back immediately that John had been hired. Of course, that didn't happen.

However, three weeks later in early August 1963, John came home from work earlier than usual and said, "Nelle, let's go to Charlotte tonight to the Open Kitchen for dinner."

I said, "Oh, John, that will cost ten dollars. It's late to get a babysitter, and I hate to ask your parents to babysit. It's so hard on them after working all day to look after all three children now. I'll make something really good for dinner."

He gave me his famous big smile and exclaimed, "But what if I told you I *got* the job at Sea Pines and Charles wants us to move as soon as possible?"

I screamed, "Well, we're definitely going out to dinner!" We were thrilled beyond words.

Moving

A whirlwind is the only way to describe the next few weeks. We began by telling the children—Gettys, six; Spencer, four; and Ora Elliott, two—that we were moving to the beach and that Gettys would get to ride a school bus to school. Spencer was jealous of that, and John's mother was naturally worried.

There we were in an huge old house that we were renovating with lots of family antiques, and we were moving (John had seen the apartment on his first visit) to a small cement-block apartment with two bedrooms, one bath, and one room that was a combination living and dining room and kitchen. (The eight villas had been built as affordable housing for Sea Pines workers.) The apartment was furnished, John said, but we'd have to take our refrigerator/freezer to put in the large closet in the entrance to the apartment. John described the kitchen as "Lilliputian in size with a mini-refrigerator underneath the sink, which has a drain the size of a quarter." There was no washer or dryer, not even in most of the rental houses then, but there was a washeteria.

However, we were so excited that even I didn't worry about those missing things. We stored our furniture in the huge basement of John's parents' house, put all that we had to take with us—clothes, a youth bed with sides for Ora because there were only twin beds in the one children's bedroom, kitchen utensils—all packed in John's parents' furniture store truck, driven by a great, strong worker from the store, Barney Anderson. And our cook and babysitter, Mary-zetter Byars, who kept the children while I taught school, came along to help, too.

My mother came to assist for a few days and sleep on the sofa while we got Gettys in school—to look after the little children and help unpack. At long last, we were off in our station wagon filled to the brim with kids and Spencer's cat, Sweetie, much like the Beverly Hillbillies!

After we went over the bridge to Hilton Head, it seemed to take forever to reach the south end of the Island. The only structures were small houses with the doors and ceilings painted blue, to keep the haunts and evil spirits away, we learned later. A small restaurant called Roadside Rest was on the left side of the road. The kids kept asking, "When are we going to get there? When can we get in the water?" We explained that we couldn't go to the beach that day because we had to unpack. My mother was very quiet, worried, I'm now sure, but she never said a negative word.

Finally, we went down a dusty road—Cordillo Road wasn't paved then—with dense foliage on either side, kind of like a Tarzan and Jane movie. All of a sudden, we saw the eight concrete-block villas seemingly cleared right out of the forest. Nothing else was on that road.

The furniture truck pulled up behind us, and Barney and Mary-zetter both looked stunned. Surely the Smiths had not moved to this. Their feelings got worse when they went inside the apartment. Maryzetter said, "Oh, Mrs. Smith, there ain't no place to put your things. No place!"

I comforted her with my excitement and hugs, saying, "It's going to be fine, Maryzetter. I promise!"

Gettys, who was hungry, said, "Daddy, where's the dining room?"

John said, "Don't worry, it's here, all in this one big room. We'll eat here, watch television here, and your mother will cook here, too. But for right now, we'll have a picnic." And out came the food Mom and I had brought along with us. The kids loved it. And then the unpacking began.

Confusion reigned, and when I had a moment to really look at the kitchen, I was reminded of a galley on a train or an airplane. It was definitely planned by a bachelor, and around five o'clock, Charles James (the bachelor who had planned it) came by to welcome us as a neighbor, as he lived in one of the apartments, too. We became great friends. As he often showed up at suppertime, I knew to cook plenty every night, because we all loved his visits so much. We needed friends.

After a long, hard day unpacking, we sadly said good-bye to Maryzetter and Barney in the Smiths' truck. I knew they were thinking: *Oh, this is the sad end of this family. They have driven their ducks to a poor market.*

First Days on the Island

Gettys

The next day, John, Gettys, and I drove to Bluffton to enroll Gettys in the first grade of school, which had already begun several days earlier. Gettys was so excited, especially over riding home on a school bus. We went shopping at the one general store, Planters Mercantile, for a broom, mop, and other little things before driving back to the Island. Bluffton seemed very far then, because there was little on either side of the road, just a small number of houses and the Roadside Rest.

Spencer

Our four-and-a-half-year-old, Spencer, was so jealous over the school bus and of Gettys getting to go to school. Every day when Gettys got home from school, he couldn't wait to ask him, "What are the new words for today?" Then he'd practice writing them over and over on his little blackboard. One day he asked Gettys, "Is there anything else you know, Gettys, that I don't know?"

Gettys laughed and exasperatedly answered, "I know too much. I can't tell you all I know!"

When Spencer turned five, he cried and begged me to call the school and talk to the teacher. "Tell her how much I know," and then he begged for me to call the principal. I hoped he would never lose that love of learning.

When John's mother called a few nights later, Gettys answered the telephone. I think she decided this was a good time to ask him a few questions because she was naturally concerned about our moving to this remote island with no doctor, and Gettys riding the school bus which came early, around 6:30 or 6:45 a.m. She asked, "Gettys, does your mother wait outside with you until the bus comes?"

He quickly said, "Oh, no, ma'am, me and Brad just throw rocks at the alligators until the bus comes." She gasped in disbelief and dropped her phone. Later she apologized to me over the phone for asking Gettys instead of asking me. This continues to be a favorite story in the family.

The little boy with Gettys was Brad Durham, who also was living in one of the apartments. His father, Travis, was an engineer overseeing some infrastructure near the William Hilton Inn. Brad is now an outstanding, well-known dentist in Savannah and Hilton Head. The Durhams became very good friends of ours, even though they didn't stay but a year on the Island.

That Sunday morning, my father came down to the Island to pick up Mother and drive back to Winnsboro, South Carolina, where I had grown up. With only my immediate family and no friends here, I felt lonely and a little abandoned. But I came to realize that this separation made us grow closer to each other. Besides, this was a new adventure and the beginning of my really growing up with no one to depend on except John and me.

Each day after seeing Gettys off to school, feeding breakfast to John, Spencer, and Ora Elliott, I would take them in our only car, still in their pajamas, to drive John to work at the small Sea Pines office. Then back to our #8 apartment to clean up, dress the kids, etc., and then head to a place where we spent a great deal of time for the next two years … the Laundromat! This was at the back of the first grocery store, where the Piggly Wiggly is now. Because I was there so much, people thought I was the attendant, as I filled up seven or eight machines, and I knew all the answers to their questions. "Where do you get change? Soap powder?" All of the answers would be the same: "At the grocery store next door." Also, I could tell people which machines, washer or dryers, worked the best, and whether they were fast or slow. As the rental homes and apartments didn't have washers and dryers either, I made some great friends there.

While the newcomers were building their houses, they had to come to the Laundromat. The Arthur Halls, the Cobby Noyes, the T. Holland Hunters, and the Curtis Henrys became my neighbors on Beach Lagoon two years later, but we began our friendships at that Laundromat.

Next door to the Laundromat was the first beauty shop, called Cha-Lo, with one lady operator, but there was no regular barber then. It was located in Coligny Plaza where the Hair Company is now.

Charles had suggested that I call Aileen McGinty for questions about anything because she and Pete had three little ones and had lived on the Island for years. So, of course, I did, and she told me that I could join other mothers at a "play-and-learning," or kindergarten group, with preschoolers twice a week from nine to twelve, if I'd be willing to take my turn at teaching them once a month.

Of course, I was so glad to know about this, because the children needed friends and learning before the first grade. Even though Ora Elliott was only two, I was allowed to bring her also, as no one had any help or family who could look after the tiny ones. The Baptist church kindly let us meet in their Sunday school rooms at their small church building, where their beautiful church stands today. Amazingly, this worked fine. Mothers and teachers brought cookies and Kool-Aid and books to read to the children, and also taught them songs, games, ABCs, how to count, and art with coloring books. All of us got to be great friends.

John's Description of Hilton Head and Sea Pines

I don't know which comes first, but about the same time Mr. Roller opened his liquor store, the Presbyterians and the Baptists started the first Island churches. The Presbyterians met in the little chapel out in a field at Honey Horn Plantation. The Baptists, by the time we moved here in 1963, had built a small church building across from the William Hilton Inn.

Sea Pines offices were housed in two small, square buildings, very much like Charles's house at Sea Pines Circle. When you drove down 278 at that time, it was a welcome sight. There were few buildings between the bridge and the circle, and there had been none for quite a few miles before reaching the circle. There was nothing between Sea Pines Circle and Coligny Circle and nothing between Sea Pines Circle and the little marina building at Palmetto Bay. The entire office population at Sea Pines consisted of a handful of people. There was Charles and Chuck James, the treasurer and sometime architect; three ladies in accounting; Herman Seimers, the vice president of operations; and myself. There were two real estate salesmen: Dave Harrell and Wally Butler.

Things were very up to date at Sea Pines by the time I arrived. We had telephones in our offices. Before I got to the Island, the only telephone at the Sea Pines office was rigged up inside the car, so that

18

when someone called, the horn blew, and everyone ran out to see who was calling or had gotten a wrong number.

The William Hilton Inn was an eighty-unit place, which was hardly more than a motel, but from the beginning was distinguished by the name of the Inn. Its Grog and Galley was the only bar on the Island and needless to say was a very popular place.

The Inn had a few weeks of good occupancy in the spring around Easter and then pretty good occupancy during the summer. After Labor Day, it could have closed its doors except for the locals in the Grog and Galley, and the dining room, which was about the only place to eat out except for the Roadside Rest.

The Inn was an afterthought of Charles's, as was the golf course. Charles wanted to develop a unique new land development project. He had spent his summers for several years during college and law school touring the beach areas of the East Coast and asking what people there would do differently if they could do it all over again. With the gleanings of all of those interviews, he put together a new concept and took it to Hideo Sasaki, who was head of landscape design at Harvard and head of his own outstanding law firm. He developed from Charles's gleanings the Sea Pines concept of cul-de-sac roads, rather than the traditional street of front-row, second-row houses, which were characteristic of other beach areas. Each street of cul-de-sacs was separated from the next by an easement and an elaborate system of foot paths, which allowed property owners to get to those easements and the beach without crossing any other property. Houses were small, simple cottages locked away in the lush natural landscape, with natural pine straw covering the ground surrounding the houses. Sea Pines Drive wound its way through clumps of the biggest and finest trees, rather than cutting them down and having a straight road.

The first time I went to New York to call on magazine editors to try to get them to write stories about Sea Pines was quite an experience. I made cold calls. They didn't know me. They had never heard of Sea Pines or Hilton Head and were not really very sure about where South Carolina was.

The reason I've been concentrating so heavily on Sea Pines at this point is that there wasn't much else here. Port Royal had a nine-hole golf course and a half dozen houses. Palmetto Dunes was a wilderness where members of the North Carolina Gun Club hunted once or twice a year. With the exception of some small communities where residents who were native to the Island lived, the remainder of the Island was all wilderness.

As I mentioned earlier, the golf courses and the Inn were afterthoughts of Charles's. He wanted a unique land development project, and that was the Sea Pines concept. People would come to the Island and fall in love with the place and buy some of the exorbitantly priced lots at five thousand or six thousand dollars each on the oceanfront. The problem was that some people would come over and look around and like what they saw, but there was no place for them to stay overnight or for a few days until Cupid struck them the fatal blow and they fell in love with the Island. The answer was an inn. Sea Pines started as a company in 1957 and the Inn in 1959 or 1960. The beach was a great attraction during the summer, but there had to be some way to lure guests here for longer periods of time. A golf course was the answer. One small tennis court was hidden away in the woods, where it was never seen or used. The Ocean Course was designed as a recreational sales tool and not as a place to add more lots. It was years before the first lot was sold along one of those fairways, and everyone was surprised when some misguided soul decided he would rather have a place along the golf course than a place along the beach. The first house built along a fairway was that of Dee and George Asnip, parents of Bill Asnip, who later moved to the Island and worked with Sea Pines. The Asnips could have bought wherever they wanted, but chose to buy several lots at the end of a strip of land near the fifteenth green on the ocean and along the sixteenth fairway. They wanted it because it was so private and removed from the other areas. It certainly was at the time. Pavement stopped along Sea Pines Drive around Beach Lagoon Road, and it was sandy lanes from there on.

John's First Meeting a Gullah Gentleman: William Aiken

1963

A tall, slender, truly black man with some facial hair was the janitor at the small Sea Pines office complex when we arrived. I spoke pleasantly with him the first time I saw him. I introduced myself and, so doing, was introduced to a pleasant, gentle man with great dignity. His name was William Aiken.

William could sweep a floor or empty a trash can in an office with the most casual dignity one can imagine. There was nothing menial about his movements. His skin was a true black color. His eyes were intelligent. His features were refined and not of the broader aspect common to many members of the Negro race. His speech was likewise, lilting pleasant and filled with dignity.

One day I asked William, "How are you doing today?"

"Just fine," he said. "Me troaty hurt."

I said, "I'm sorry, I didn't understand what you said."

He said, "Except me troaty hurt."

I did not want to appear rude or stupid, so I asked the third time and the third time he repeated, "My throat, he hurts." Finally, my ear adjusted to the lilting patois and I discerned what he was saying. The Gullah uses "he" instead of "it" or "she" as a matter of fact.

John's Efforts to Start a School on the South End

1965–1966

There were only a handful of families on the south end of the Island with school-age children in the mid-1960s. Most of us worked for Sea Pines in one way or another. Our children were bused to Bluffton for elementary and high school. My own children would leave in the dark in the morning and return after dark at night. We were also confronted in this part of the country at that time with total integration of the public schools. The white population on Hilton Head was a small minority, and basically the same was true for all lower Beaufort County. Our community on Hilton Head was interested in a high-quality school to prepare our children for colleges. All of our community were college graduates, and that educational level was in an extremely small percentage in the remainder of the area. My idea was to try for a public school somewhere on the southern end of Hilton Head. My wife and I got a group of concerned parents together and made a formal request to the school board and contacted our delegate to the House of Representatives. We also felt it would be a good addition to our cause if we had someone on the county school board. I ran for the office and miraculously was elected—the first person from the Island to be elected to a county office in many, many years. It didn't do us any good, however. We had already been turned down for our school.

I, then, came up with the idea of a private school. I talked to Charles Fraser about this and told him a school was essential to retain the people he needed on the Island to develop and operate the company. He agreed, and with that authorized for the Sea Pines Company to financially back a private school. At that point, we had about three or four months before the new school year should begin. I called a meeting of all the parents we could round up who had elementary-age children. We found several of these were either lukewarm or opposed to a private school. Bluffton was getting a new gym that year, and some thought that was the most important ingredient in staying there. We decided we would go ahead with or without those families. With Sea Pines financing, I hired Dr. McCormack, the retired head of Chatham County Schools in Savannah, who was living in Bluffton as a consultant. I worked with him for several weeks on basic needs and then with Tom Triol, headmaster of Savannah Country Day, on particulars for a private school and recommendations for a headmaster. Actually, he recommended a headmistress, Lillian Goddard, who had taught at his school for a number of years and who was interested in a new challenge. We certainly provided her some.

Meanwhile, Harold Depkin, who was also a vice president of Sea Pines and had worked with a private school starting in Roanoke, Virginia, was in charge of the physical plan for the school. We had determined that the original Baptist church, which is still located on the site of the present new building, would be the best one for our private school. Harold was getting the necessary partitions put in, ordering desks and other equipment. We both met and agreed to hire Lillian Goddard as headmistress, and then I met with her to interview several teachers. We interviewed two beautiful young ladies from Savannah, who had graduated from Country Day

Sea Pines Academy official opening.

before college. We opened for our first day of school only two days later than we had originally announced. When we held a flag raising ceremony at the front of the school, before going inside for a short opening ceremony, the flagpole was still lying on the ground beside the hole that was prepared for it. I got a couple of other people to help me set it in place, and then we grabbed one of the children to raise the flag.

John's Marketing Plans for Golf

The first big athletic event that took place on the Island was an exhibition match with Bruce Devlin and Jack Nicklaus. I had signed Bruce's contract as a touring pro a few months earlier. He was the first big-name athlete associated with the Island. The exhibition match was played on the Ocean Course, and it was a big thing on the Island with all of us who were involved. We wore pith helmets to distinguish us from other people who came to see the stars.

We were building a second golf course by that time, and that's when we learned that Jack was interested in building golf courses. The excitement of that first exhibition match generated the germ of an idea for a tournament. We couldn't have one with only one course, since it would cut off play for our members and guests. As the Sea Marsh course was not a tournament course, we thought we'd put off ideas of a tournament until we had a third course. Charles, Donald O'Quinn, and I met with Jack at the Masters and discussed a new course. There was verbal agreement on his participation, but Jack was not an architect. Pete Dye had built a good new course somewhere that was attracting some attention. So with Jack's suggestion or blessing, we went to Pete. We worked out an agreement that Jack and Pete would collaborate on the new course in Sea Pines, and the idea of a tournament was ready to be pursued. I recall the details of organizing this event in the published story that follows, "The Heritage, It's Festive and Fun."

The first Heritage was played Thanksgiving week of 1969. The golf course was finished just in time for the opening play. The clubhouse still had painters and carpet layers in it when the pros showed up to check in before the tournament began. On opening day, everything was finished.

Fortunately, Arnold Palmer won that first Heritage. Based on particulars about America's first golf course—founded in 1786 in Charleston—I selected red jackets for committee people, choosing the red jackets worn by players in the eighteenth-century prints. My suggested name, the Heritage, was the one we used for the tournament. We also used the ancient opening rites of the St. Andrews Tournament, the cannon firing while the defending champion hit the first ball. Charles wanted the bagpipers, and so they became a part of the Heritage, I'm happy to say. Pete and Jack's golf course won raves. And the Heritage was launched.

Sports Illustrated came back and did a five- or six-page feature on the Harbour Town Course. *Golf* and *Golf Digest* did similar features. The course was picked by *Golf* as one of the top twenty courses in the world its first year. It was a decision that still gives them grief. No other course has ever been selected when it was so young.

I was privileged to be chairman of the Heritage for the next five years. Sea Pines became well-established in golf. A golf-playing president, Dwight D. Eisenhower, did a lot to popularize it, and it was Palmer's decade.

First Annual

Heritage Golf Classic

November 24 - 30, 1969

THE PLANTATION CLUB

HILTON HEAD ISLAND, SOUTH CAROLINA

GENERAL INFORMATION

First Annual Heritage Golf Classic brochure

Ticket sales will be limited to 5,000 ad-
missions. No daily tickets sold.

GROUNDS ONLY SEASON TICKETS
One badge for admission to course and
grounds for full week of play. Also includes parking and copy of annual...
@ $20.00 Each $_____

CLUBHOUSE AND GROUNDS
SEASON TICKETS
One badge for Clubhouse admission for
full week of play, which includes both
the Clubhouse and beautiful Lakehouse
area next to the Clubhouse. Also includes parking and copy of annual...
@ $30.00 Each $_____

PATRON PLAN
On Patron Badge, one preferred parking sticker, six (6) season grounds and
Clubhouse guest badges and listing on
the patron board and copy of annual...
@$150.00 Each$_____

PRO-AM CONTESTANT PLAN
Each participant in the Pro-Am Tournament will receive a Pro-Am player badge
for admittance to grounds and Clubhouse.
One preferred parking sticker, plus four
(4) season grounds and Clubhouse badges
and copy of annual...
@$225.00 Each$_____

Enclosed is my check or money order for:
Total: $_____

All Checks Payable to Heritage Golf Classic

Name_____

Address_____

City_____State_____Zip_____

Mail order and check to:
Heritage Golf Classic
Sea Pines Plantation Club
Hilton Head Island, S. C. 29928

Heritage Golf Tournament ticket order form

The Heritage: It's Festive and Fun

Written by John Gettys Smith, 1969;
published in Islander Magazine, *1980*

March is a time of much doing around our Island. Everything and everyone seems to be into a fit of activity. It is Hilton Head's annual rite of spring, and it involves not just the cascades of pastel blooms that ornament almost every vista. Hundreds of Islanders deck themselves out in bright red, green and yellow arranged in a pattern that originated far from our shores on craggy cliffs and moors of old Scotland. The people's colors are laid out in a precise pattern almost identical to a design of the Royal House of Stuart whose descendants today sit on the throne of Great Britain and most thrones which remain occupied or pretend to in Europe. Only a yellow bar is a variation from the Stuart tartan to make the Heritage tartan distinctive.

March is the month when the heritage of golf, both at its birthplace in Scotland and America, is heralded here. The first golf club in America was at Charleston in 1786. It is the month of the Heritage Golf Classic, today one of this country's most august tournaments. It has come a long way since the inaugural Heritage was played during the first cold week of November in 1969. Summer had stayed with us right up to Thanksgiving week that year. Summer flowers were still blooming and had been joined by bright chrysanthemums which could wait no longer for brisker fall weather to come. Summer grass was lush and the very new fairways and greens of the Harbour Town Golf Links were bright with rye to add color and substance to the rather thin carpet of Tifton which was supposed to cover them.

The temperatures were still in the balmy mid-seventies as they had been since early October. It had to end sometime. It chose the evening prior to the first opening parade, which that year began on the 18th green and marched to the practice range at the still-being-completed Clubhouse. Hammers punctuated the sound of bagpipes as the little columns of flagbearers, officials and committee people marched toward they were not sure what.

The temperature had started to drop with the sun on the previous evening. The wind had come up during the night and had developed into a full-fledged nor'easter by mid-afternoon and parade time. Parkas and scarves replaced short sleeves of the previous afternoon.

The unpopular yellow jackets for V.I.P.'s which had been prematurely ordered during the spring planning period were Palm Beach thin. Why yellow? Why summer weight and that color for a Thanksgiving week event? There was no reason due to heritage. The first director of the tournament liked that color. He was about the only one who admired it, and the following years hence the red jacket reminiscent of the old golfing print used for the tournament's logo has been the official jacket.

Despite the cold north winds that blew, the parade was a success. Jack Nicklaus had been invited to act as Captain of Gentlemen Golfers, borrowed from early Scottish tournaments, and hit the first ball to officially launch the Heritage. There was, of course, no previous winner that first year, and since Jack had worked with course designer Pete Dye to create the Harbour Town Links from the tropical wilderness it had been, he was a logical selection.

Jack had climbed to the pinnacle of golfdom by 1969, but he had never synchronized his golf swing with a blast from a Revolutionary War–era cannon, which was made an instant tradition at the Heritage. It recalls the early tournaments in Scotland where this was the custom. Jack was in the midst of his backswing when the cannon fired somewhat prematurely. Jack instantly proved himself an all-round athlete. He did something akin to a high jump–broad jump–sprint from the tee. When the smoke from the gunpowder cleared and the clustered spectators reopened their own eyes and uncovered their ears, only the still-in-place ball and hastily discarded club remained where once the mighty golfer had so recently been.

The little gallery loved it! Great laughter and a round of applause encouraged Jack to resume his stance. With his characteristic grin and twinkle he hesitantly reassumed the ready position. Then came the roll of the drum from the pipers' band, the backswing and a perfectly coordinated blast and shot. The master had reassumed his image and the ball flew away somewhere in the direction of the beach. A cheer went up, champagne corks popped and the official hostesses, wives of Heritage officials, passed out complimentary wine to the spectators.

That night there was a hard freeze. It was a very hard freeze. Sunrise found not only the limp, dead stems of summer flowers but the frozen solid greens at Harbour Town. The first Pro-Am did not get off to a roaring start. It almost did not get off at all. Players could not be permitted to walk on the greens due to their frozen condition and the resulting killing of the tender grass.

Play did not begin until almost midday, and there was only time for nine holes before it became dark. Despite it all, the Pro-Am and the tournament came off beautifully with a fine field of golfers.

Jack Nicklaus and Arnold Palmer led the list of the illustrious.

Arnold had not won a tournament in 14 months. He was the subject of a cover story that very month in *Golf* magazine which deposed the king and called it the end of his era.

A good turnout of sportswriters assured the tournament of some good exposure. Dan Jenkins, the great *Sports Illustrated* editor-author, was on hand due to special invitations from his friend Charlie Price and myself. Dan really did not expect to have much to write about since his magazine does not usually cover brand-new tournaments that fall below the top purse events. At several points in time the leaderboards listed a group of names virtually unknown outside their own family connections. They were hardly household words nor likely to become so if they won the inaugural Heritage.

Sunday came and with it a clear, cool day for the final round. It had been a good tournament so far, but nothing to make it a great one. There were the Heritage trimmings to give spectacle, but nothing to make the event really spectacular. There were a lot of good golfers out there playing good games. No one was tearing up the course, we were glad about that one. But there was nothing to really shout about and give the Heritage a big boost.

That is, not until the afternoon began to move into its higher numerals. Then from out of the pack came the big man himself. A memorable event was in the making as he charged through the back nine and into the long stretch of the 17th and 18th with an unfinished lighthouse waiting behind a growing gallery ringing the final green.

Arnie's Army swarmed behind him and ran for positions to watch him putt out and finish. It was too good to be true! The old sureness had been regained, and Arnold marched down that long sweep of green closer to a victory than he had been in far too many painful months. It had eluded him before. A swell of applause carried him onto the green and he lifted his cap and smiled upon his fans. At this point, virtually everyone there fell into that category, and he knew it. The Army was intact. Its leader was *the* leader.

I almost missed the winning putt as I signaled "no" to the bag-pipers who were poised, pipes to mouths and hands to drumsticks, ready to play. I indicated to them that one small premature squeak from any one of them would result in my personally cutting off their wind forever. I turned back to the man of the moment just in time to see the ball roll swiftly across the green and fall with absolute finality into the cup. The pipers broke into play on cue, Arnold jumped with obvious joy, and Dan Jenkins could now write a piece about Arnold winning on the course that Jack built.

There was a very brief ceremony on the green as Charles Fraser, Donald O'Quinn, and I rushed over to congratulate the winner. I introduced Charles, who thanked the gallery and the players. I then introduced Jack Nicklaus and Pete Dye as the men responsible for the design of the course. (I was so excited I introduced Jack as "Nicklaus!") They both spoke a few words, and then it was time to introduce the Great Man himself.

He warmly called his victory at the Heritage as important as any in his career. It was a statement guaranteed to warm the cockles of tournament officials' hearts and spoken with a graciousness and sincerity that clouded many an eye. He then donned the winner's jacket, and the first Heritage was history.

The list of Islanders who have worked as committee chairmen and chairwomen is legion. Some fine stalwarts have worked … and it *is* work … in every Heritage since 1969. Others have joined this supportive group in more recent years. Without them the tourna-ment could never have been played. There were times at the very beginning when it seemed it would not.

The first meeting to organize community participation for the planned event was in my office at the Sea Pines headquarters complex. A handful of people were there for it. They included General Ted Timberlake, Buddy McDill and Julian Heron as well as our tournament director, Bill Dyer, Don O'Quinn, then the vice president for maintenance and construction and assistant chairman for the proposed event and myself.

As I may have mentioned previously, almost immediately there was dissension within the gathering. To say that our tournament director and our absolutely essential committee people did not hit it off—well—would be a major understatement. The meeting was hardly begun before the temperature in the room began to rise. One word led to another, and I was not sure it was not going to lead to more than words.

We cut it short to avoid a walkout by the potential committee chairman. There were some very obvious differences of opinion as well as some mutual lack of confidence between residents and our director. After the heating up within the gathering, things became very chilly. The three gentlemen representing residents left the room, but Julian returned momentarily as he said "to close the door to the refrigerator." I went directly to Charles and told him about the near disaster in the meeting and suggested we needed to have someone as a consultant to the tournament who could command respect from our residents and the tournament director, none of whom had ever run a major PGA event. In fact, no one involved had those credentials. Tournament directors can be replaced no matter how painful the process might be. Residents cannot be.

Charles agreed to the need, and I suggested Charlie Price, founding editor of *Golf* magazine, author of a book on golf history, writer of a monthly golf column etc., etc. I then went to New York to try to convince Charlie to join us. It certainly was no easy task. I went to Charlie's jazzy Upper East Side apartment to try to carry out this chore. Charlie let me know immediately, in an unmistakable tone, that he was a city boy born and bred and chose to remain one. The thought of living on some remote island, which surely must be mainly inhabited by creepy crawling things on the ground and yellow fever bearing things in the air, had absolutely no appeal to the man sitting there in his sky-lighted and tailored pad in the East 70s.

He did not own, drive, or want to have either of those relationships with a car. I knew I could not lie about the ready availability of taxis on Hilton Head. I offered him a car, bed and board, plus all the golf he could play at our expense for a six-month term of consulting. When I left him that afternoon, I was really not very sure I'd ever hear from him, even on a Christmas card, again. However, we had another chat or two by telephone and miraculously he agreed to make the move down to the Island.

Even after Charlie became a transplant, I had moments when I thought we would lose him. One of these was not too many days after he arrived. He needed a haircut and he was running out of the fancy little cigars which he required to keep him off cigarettes. Needless to say, an Island that had no barber had no such cigars.

I took him to Savannah to prove that civilization—something akin to it as he had known it—was only an hour away. I really should not have worried about it. Something bit Charlie all right. The love bug got him and got him good. Charlie fell head over heels in love with Hilton Head Island. He determined never to leave it again. He's kept that promise to himself with only short excursions to the Masters, to accept an invitation or two from King Hassan of Morocco to be among his guests for a few days, and a few exotic whirls around the world to collect material for some travel-golf pieces he was asked to write for magazines.

One of the busiest Islanders this month is also occupied with the Heritage year-round. Bonnie Hunt became the first tournament secretary for the Heritage in January 1970, following the first Heritage two months earlier. There was no special secretary for the first event, with my secretary and Donald O'Quinn's doing those honors. It was obvious after that first go-round there needed to be a full-time person for that post as well a keeper of the central files for the tournament. The Heritage files were moved from my office to the offices in the Harbour Town Clubhouse and have remained there, with a couple of moves out and back, ever since.

"They've moved us a couple of times, but they always end up moving us back here," Bonnie said. Bonnie efficiently runs the Heritage office. If she has ever been ruffled or lost her poise, I've neither seen it nor heard about it. She moves about quietly getting things done.

Tournament directors over the past decade have been Bill Dyer, 1969; Dave Albaugh, 1970 and '71; Justin Jenkins, 1972 and '73; Bud Bowie, 1974 and '75; and Bill Carson, 1976, '77, '78 and '79. Bill had been involved with the Heritage from the beginning when he was greenskeeper and responsible for getting the Harbour Town Course ready for play.

Sonny Graham is director for the first time this year. However, Sonny also has been involved with the Heritage from the first year. He was in charge of communications for a number of years and was Bill Carson's assistant last year.

The second year of the Heritage, the speaker for the PA system was hung in a tree some distance from the presentation stand. It faced back toward the stand. I checked it with a few taps to be sure the mike was working and then started the awards ceremonies. I began making my welcoming remarks to the assembled gallery. It seemed for a few seconds there was no sound and then it started coming back at me from the box in the tree along the fairway. It was like a delayed echo. I was hearing myself speak the just-spoken words but about a dozen words later. It was really frustrating at first until I was able to tune it out in my mind by concentrating as hard as possible on what I was about to say rather than what had just been said.

Without a long list of really dedicated workers the Heritage could never operate with the smoothness it does. Hundreds of Islanders contribute their time and very considerable talents to make it one of the most finely tuned tournaments in the world. A number of these people have been committee chairmen since the first tournament; dozens of others have worked on those committees for all of those years. They have been augmented by large numbers of newer residents who have caught the spirit of the Heritage and volunteer to keep making it a great tournament and aid in making it even better.

Buddy McDill has been a vital part of the tournament since that very first meeting in my office back in 1968 when we began the community participation planning for the 1969 tournament. Buddy is overall chairman for all the men volunteers. Vi Vilas is his counterpart for the women. Vi has worked for the Heritage from the beginning and replaced longtime Ladies Chairman Mary Ellen Mulford in that position when she moved from the Island several years ago. Here are some of the key chairmen:

Buddy McDill—General Chairman of Men Volunteers
Bob Killingsworth—General Vice Chairman of Men
Art Hedeman—Chairman of Parking
Alonzo Giles—Chairman of Caddies
Phil Bachelder—Chairman of Scoring
Bill Cole—Co-chairman of Scoring

Tom Wilson—Chairman for Press

Fred Wilkins—Chairman for Opening Ceremonies

Karl Kellerman—Chairman of Marshals

Bill Creech—Chairman of Lighting

Vance Fowler and Leo Beckman—Announcer at #9 and #18
holes respectively

Mrs. R. A. Vilas—General Chairman of Ladies Volunteers

Mrs. Robert McDuffie and Mrs. Joseph Borders—Apparel
Chairmen

Mrs. Art Hedeman—Chairman for Information

Mrs. Clarence Hatch and Mrs. Karl Kellerman—Chairmen of
Transportation

Mrs. Tom Wilson and Mrs. James Cowie—Chairmen of
Registration

Mrs. Tom Williams and Mrs. Vance Fowler—Chairmen of
Markers

Mrs. N. J. Dawson—Scoreboard

It is impossible to include all of the volunteers who staff vital jobs and who have been longtime Heritage workers. They may be unsung but never unappreciated heroes of the Heritage.

Sonny, Bonnie and two secretaries are year-round employees for the Heritage. At tournament time, the staff is beefed up by part-time helpers. These are usually college-age young men. One of these is now post-college but continues to come back every year and serve as a runner for the Heritage office. He is Mitch Palles, who is a banker in Florence, but arranges his annual vacation time to coincide with the Heritage so he can continue being a part of it.

The Heritage is the biggest event held each year on the Island. It draws thousands of people from all over the country to watch the world's top golfers play on one of the world's greatest courses in an atmosphere often referred to as "clubby." Originally, we limited the gallery to no more than 5,000 people. In those days members of the gallery could well find themselves one of a half-dozen spectators watching one of the most famous names in the sport putt out on a green.

Parking was not so much of a problem with that size gallery. Restaurants, bars and private parties were filled in the evenings with celebrating Islanders and visitors, but they were not overcrowded. Almost everyone on the Island was a Heritage participant in some way when the tournament was played Thanksgiving week. To secure television coverage it was necessary to move the tournament to its present slot in the spring. It comes at a time of peak occupancy even if the tournament was not being played. Therefore, the Island hits a high point of people count during Heritage Week. It's a wonderful time. It's festive and fun. Everyone seems to be doing something, but if it's the only time you are a part-time Islander, you really owe it to yourself to come back when things are more leisurely. May and October are particularly delightful months, but then so are the other ten.

John's Ideas to Promote Tennis, Too

By 1970, it seemed to me it was time for a new big sport to emerge, and a feature story in *Time* pointed out several new members of the administration in Washington did not play golf, but were tennis players. I got interested and began to check every magazine I could lay my hands on. Several of them had little tidbits about tennis players. It was something new. No one had written anything about tennis except maybe Wimbledon or the U.S. Open. I talked to Charles about tennis and sent him some of the magazines marked in red, along with my scientifically tested theory that tennis was to be the next big sport. Charles is an innovator, so he didn't say I was crazy. When I suggested we build some new courts, however, he said, "No one plays on the one we already have."

I reminded him that we had never pushed tennis in anything we had ever done in marketing. No one knew that our court was hidden in the woods. Tennis courts would give Sea Pines a little extra jazz. Charles agreed reluctantly to build four hard-surface courts. I also got him to hire our first pro, Pete Collins, a young guy from Savannah who played tennis. I couldn't get agreement to give him a Pro Shop. Golf was our game. Our pro operated for several months using the trunk of his car for storage and a poolside table with an umbrella as his office adjacent to the courts. I thought I'd performed a miracle when I convinced Charles and Don O'Quinn, who by this time was in charge of sports, which was really just golf, to build a

Pro Shop there. It was only about four by six, had a door but no windows; but it was the Pro Shop. They use it as a storage room at the Harbour Town courts now. Despite our meager facilities, we still had more courts (even if they were hard ones) than most resorts at the time. I learned people really wanted to play on a soft surface, and when we were ready to add some more courts, and a new location at Harbour Town, we put in six clay, or Har-Tru, ones. With this many courts, we were getting the attention of people who were also in the forefront of the tennis boom. Donald Dell and Frank Craighill, from Washington, were into tennis. Donald had been on our Davis Cup team and was an attorney. He was promoting tennis players the way Mark McCormack had been promoting golfers. He suggested to me that a bright young and promising player would be an asset for us and possibly lead to a tournament in Sea Pines. The guy's name was Stan Smith, and he was still serving his military duty in the army. The stars of the sport were not household names across the country then. The sport of tennis, at that time, was granted very few lines on the sports pages of daily newspapers. (All that was about to change.)

I asked Stan Smith to come down for an interview and immediately liked him. He seemed to me to fit the Sea Pines image for a touring pro to a T. He was a tall, good-looking man, rather shy, very polite, and a nice young gentleman.

In May 1971, Charles said that I had his permission to sign Stan's contract to be the first Sea Pines Tennis Touring Pro, one of the first of this breed at any resort.

In June, it looked as if we were going to be the site for a CBS network televised tournament, yet to be named.

Stan was still in the army but was going to be able to play at Wimbledon. Knowing that Wimbledon was the finest venue for a tennis tournament in the world, I deemed it appropriate to go there and

John Gettys Smith, Pete Collins, first tennis pro, and Stan Smith, the first touring pro, on the tennis court.

see how they did it. Charles always agreed to learn from the best in every endeavor.

I had never been to a tennis tournament in my life, and neither had anyone else with the Sea Pines Company. I made a call to Donald Dell to learn where many of the players were staying, and even at that late date they were able to get me booked into the same hotel. This proved to be a godsend in many ways. Each day a limousine picked a few of us up at the hotel and we were off to Wimbledon. The first day, Arthur Ashe was among the group. Riding out with Donald was the ideal way to go. We were unloaded at the gates and were told to meet back there after the matches in the evening.

Because of Dell and Craighill and my newfound friend, Stan Smith—no kin—I was treated to a real trip to the inner sanctum. I sat in players' seats on center court. I was free to roam the grounds, and I also had access to the men's locker room and was invited there by Stan. Several tennis writers I knew were at the players' tea room, and I began the word about Stan being our new tennis pro, and they began the process of helping me spread the word to the other media that Stan Smith of Pasadena, California, was now Stan Smith of Sea Pines on Hilton Head, South Carolina. The transfer, I was told, was not going to be easy. With their help, however, it was accomplished in pretty rapid order. I got Stan registered to vote in South Carolina, which made him officially a South Carolinian and not just a paid representative of Sea Pines whose checks came from there.

Wimbledon is an amazing place and unquestionably the best-run tournament of any variety—anywhere in the world. The British excitement over the tennis world's being focused on their lawn and tennis club was refreshing. Roses bloomed around the grounds as they would around someone's treasured home. The place is beautiful, with flowers, hedges, and ivy on the center court. They've been playing there for a long time.

I had conceived and built in many of the unique features that made the Heritage Golf Tournament distinctive and now I wanted to try to do the same for our tennis tournament. I learned during Wimbledon that this was to be a reality. Sea Pines was going to have a CBS network televised tournament. A great surprise was that we had little more than six weeks to get ready for it. One cannot grow a garden in six weeks! That was one of the distinctive features about the Wimbledon experience, in addition to the excellently run tournament itself, and the best tennis players in the world.

The idea came to me that while we couldn't grow a garden in six weeks, we could surely have planter boxes made and filled with living plants and flowers within that timeframe. I did a sketch of the simple planter boxes and could hardly wait to get them to Tom Norby in Sea Pines to have them made.

When we held that first CBS Tournament of Champions, often called WCT (World Championship Tennis), the planter boxes lined the courts for the first time in tennis history. Several of the players commented to me that I must be out of my mind, that they might break their necks falling over them. Fortunately, that did not happen. Also, very fortunately, they dressed the courts up beautifully and looked great on TV. It became a tradition at Sea Pines for all subsequent tournaments, and as a result, flowers appeared at other tennis court stadiums around the world.

Our ushers in the stadium wore uniform tennis dresses. For the Governor, Charles Fraser, for a few dignitaries, and myself, I selected green jackets, white pants, white shoes, and blue ties with crossed rackets. I got the United States Marine Corps Band from Parris Island to play a concert behind the baseline before the final, and they marched onto the court to play the national anthem of the winner immediately after the last ball had been hit in the final set. Simultaneously, flags representing each participant in the tournament were carried on court, held by ball boys and girls, and lined along the net. Then the officials proceeded to march onto the court to present checks and trophies, as the band struck up the national anthem of the winner.

The first year, in August 1971, the tennis tournament produced only a handful of spectators except for the finale. Earlier in the week when CBS was filming the early rounds, the stands were virtually empty. I called Sea Pines Academy and spoke with Lillian Goddard, our headmistress. My problem was no people. We decided the children at Sea Pines Academy would benefit from the exposure to some of the greatest tennis players in the world and decided school would let out early so that they could come and fill at least a section of the stands. The stadium was so empty that we had students and a few spectators, including complimentary tickets given to members of the Marine Corps Band and their families, to shift *ends* as the camera shifted and players changed sides. We did not want the stadium to appear empty, and it was the only way we could fill it. There was a mad dash, back and forth, and luckily the camera angles were not very imaginative in those early tournaments. Only the careful observer would realize these fans were all the same people.

When Rod Laver won the last point and became the first champion of the CBS Tournament of Champions or the WCT, the Marine Corps Band was lined up and ready for their entry. It worked like clockwork. They were followed immediately by the flag bearers with their flags and then the dignitaries, the Governor, Charles, and me. When the band played the first notes of "God Save the Queen," no one in the stands moved or even seemed to breathe. Jim Light leaned out of the stands as we were exiting after the ceremony and said to me, "Oh, John, you did it again—an instant success and tradition." Jim and I were competitive in the Sea Pines Company at the time and were not exactly the best of friends. I was touched because of his spontaneous compliment. I still have difficulty telling about the compliment, even though it has been some thirty-odd years or so.

One funny thing happened on the courts during the dignified award ceremony. Our daughter, Ora Elliott, was one of the flag bearers because she was a fledgling tennis player at the time, as were all of our ball boys and girls. Right in the middle of the ceremony, her flag fell off its staff. Bill Thomas, standing next to her and being a young Southern gentleman, handed his flag to Thornton Withers, on his other side, and proceeded in a gentlemanly and efficient way to place the flag back on its staff. He then turned, took back his own flagpole, and the ceremony moved flawlessly. Few people saw this chivalrous act because of all the court activity at the time, but those who did had difficulty in restraining themselves from congratulatory applause.

CBS was so pleased with the reception of their first televised venture that they decided immediately to return for a spring fling, less than six months away. A six months' time period seemed almost excessive to me after everything we had to do in less than six weeks for the first tournament. CBS still wanted to call the tournament the

Flag bearers for the WCT Tournament.

Tennis Masters, but the hierarchy for the Masters golf tournament would not allow it. We bandied about and one of us, I'm not sure who, came up with CBS Tennis Classic. It was *simple*—and it said what we wanted it to say. Obviously, Tournament of Tennis Champions was a little cumbersome. The first CBS Tournament of Tennis Champions had been played, canned, and then aired over several weekends. Needless to say, everyone at Sea Pines was pleased to see themselves on network television and that the tournament was being played on Hilton Head Island. I had very little success with getting Sea Pines' name before such a wide audience before that first tournament. We tried signs on the court, near the court, or wherever they seemed to be likely to be picked up and not be offensive, but CBS managed to miss most of them. They did show the scoreboard with Sea Pines Plantation.

For the first CBS Tennis Classic, I had some plans for considerably wider exposure for Sea Pines. I came up with the idea of a helicopter flying over Harbour Town taking film as it flew over the harbor and then zooming in on our stadium court. I had to convince all those involved that this was a good idea. Tennis was brand-new on network TV, except showing a few highlights at Wimbledon, the U.S. Open, the Australian Open, and the French Open. I, first, had to convince Charles Fraser of Phase I of my plan: to pay CBS for the film, if they would shoot it, and use it during the televised airing of the tournament. Charles was somewhat reluctant, but I got him to agree that we would pay up to, but not a dime more than $5,385 for the film. With this commitment, I went to CBS and made my pitch to them. They thought it was a great idea and they paid for the helicopter and the film crew—pennies spent in *promotion* that must rank as the world's best buy.

For several weekends, I believe four, CBS showed the canned segments of the tournament leading up to the finals. Each segment began with this beautiful shot from the helicopter approaching the lighthouse at Harbour Town, flying over the yacht basin and the elegant little shops and villas surrounding it, and then next door to the racquet club where they zeroed in on the court. At the end of each televised segment, they reversed the film and flew out from center court over Harbour Town. Five thousand dollars, and how many millions of people were exposed to it?

At the finals for that first CBS Tennis Classic, we had two Aussies remaining, John Newcombe and Rod Laver. On Sunday as they warmed up, the Marine Corps Band was playing its pre-final concert from behind the baseline under the camera. Over the PA system, I asked John and Rod what they would like the band to play. Simultaneously they chorused, "Waltzing Matilda." The Marine Corps Band from Parris Island was up to the task and immediately launched into a very spirited version of the favorite Australian song. John and Rod continued warming up for a few minutes and then John propped his racquet against the net, went over, and took the baton from the band director's hand and began to conduct the band. The galleries loved it. Cheers and applause rang out. This early era in the rise of tennis popularity produced an abundance of great guys.

A good percentage of the top men players at the time were Australian, and I got to know most of them pretty well. They reminded me very much of Southerners I had grown up with all my life. They were party boys, fraternity brothers in many ways. They had a good time, and they did not take themselves seriously, despite the fact that some of their records still stand after all of these years. These players for the first CBS Tournament of Tennis Champions were the top eight men in the world. Most were also included in the group "The Handsome Eight," as they were sometimes called.

One of these guys, not an American, and I planned to meet at the

Quarterdeck after one of the matches for a cold beer. All of them seemed capable and determined to drink as much cold beer as possible. This was a facet of their personalities that appealed to me greatly at the time. This player finished his match, showered and came over to the Quarterdeck looking all "squeaky clean" and very dashing. I was sitting at the bar talking with a young, attractive secretary who worked in an office on the Island when he came in. He came over to us. She looked at him. He looked at her. I introduced them and they said hello to each other and I believe broke the world's record for a quick pickup. They were out of there within a minute and a half. The player returned an hour later and rejoined me at the bar. No mention was made of the recent encounter other than he said, "Thank you for the introduction."

Actually, the players *were* gentlemen in those days. The players made so little money that they stayed with families when they were on the tour. The tour had been before resorts became involved, mainly at country clubs and club facilities around this country and the world. Because they were staying in private homes as house guests, they had to be on their good behavior, perhaps best behavior. They were charming guys to begin with and whether the manners were taught at Mother's knee or not, they soon acquired them because those with poor manners, bad habits, and bad house-guest habits ran the risk of not being invited back the next time. These were the top players at the time, I'm talking about Rod Laver, Roy Emerson, Ken Rosewall, Roger Tayor, John Newcombe, and, of course, our Stan Smith. They were top guys on the tour, and the purses at that time were so small and the endorsements so meager that they needed to be house guests in order to be able to stay on the tour.

I arranged housing for the players during that first tournament, and some of them struck up great friendships with their hosts, which endured throughout the years that Sea Pines hosted the major tennis tournaments and, in some cases, thereafter. My wife, Nelle, and I hosted a party for players, dignitaries, sponsors when there were any, and some of our friends for each and every tournament. The first one, we held at Turtle Lane Cabanas, which was a block or so from our house on Beach Lagoon Road. Turtle Lane was an oceanfront facility that was owned by Sea Pines Company. It was designed to be a small, quiet, beachside facility sitting behind the dunes in a natural landscape. It consisted of nothing more than a few wooden decks and a small restroom building and a larger open-air pavilion nearby. I had a small combo for that first party, lots of beer and booze, as well as some substantial food. The players all came— in fact, I believe everyone who was invited came. And stayed. The players danced the night away with guest ladies, who enjoyed dancing with such sports celebrities and charmers.

NBC Family Circle Tennis Tournament

APRIL 30–MAY 6, 1973

All three of the tennis tournaments, the WCT and two CBS Tennis Classics, paved the way for John to secure the Family Circle Tennis Tournament. This became so popular for twenty-seven years. Remarkably, in 1973, this was the first women's event to be broadcast on network television.

Two Californians, Jack Jones and John Moreno, were the cofounders of the tournament. They had almost chosen another resort to host the event until they came to Sea Pines. Sixteen top women pros competed for the largest first prize ever offered to a *woman* in sports—$30,000. The total purse prize money was $100,000, but it was divided to allow $30,000 for the winner. Second-place prize was $12,200. In addition to the prize money, the winner would receive a beautiful Waterford crystal cup. *Family Circle* magazine editor Robert Young and his staff, especially Merry Kelly, worked closely with Jack Jones, John Moreno, and John and his office staff. It was an incredibly busy time, but so rewarding for the women pros who played and inspiring for women all over the United States. They were deserving of the same amount of prize money as the men, and this tournament paved the way for them.

Among the top players who competed in the first Family Circle Cup were Billie Jean King, Margaret Court, Rosemary (Rosie)

Casals, Francoise Durr, Wendy Overton, Julie Heldman, Nancy Gunter Richey, Kerry Melville, and Betty Stove.

The final match was between Rosie Casals and Nancy Richey, which Rosie won. Billie Jean King remarked, "This final was not the best played match due to the nervousness of both players, but every player there that day knew that it was a historic day in women's sports."

These tournaments were the *beginning* of the $776,000 purse now played in Charleston, South Carolina. It is the oldest professional women's tournament in the United States.

I understand why the Family Circle moved to Charleston, and I love Charleston, but I feel it's a shame that Sea Pines lost it. The intimacy of our stadium, nestled there in the beauty of nature with birds chirping, was incredible.

My John also felt it was a very sad thing to lose the tournament and wrote in the *Island Packet*, "Development on the Island is relatively new. There are few traditions with very deep roots, and it is always painful to have one pulled up and lost."

But there will always be the deep roots in the minds of tennis fans of Hilton Head Island and world-class tennis events.

Nelle's Tennis Memories

I must confess that I was a perpetual beginner at tennis, but how I loved the game and the friends I made. I was the brunt of many stories about my ineptness! The worst one was that I talked and apologized to the ball machine (which mechanically shot out balls for me to return when I was practicing) when I missed a shot, saying, "Oh, I'm so sorry." Friends loved teasing me about this and declare that it was true. I hope not.

Being one of the volunteers at each tennis tournament—the WCT, the two CBS Tennis Classics, and the Family Circle Tennis Tournament—was so much fun. Mainly, we hostess ladies welcomed and directed ticket holders to their seats, and controlled the crowd from going in and out during play. We wore identical white tennis dresses that were chosen for each tournament. We looked forward to each new outfit.

I was even on a local women's tennis team, playing one day a week at 8:30 a.m. One day, I was running late and dressed rather hurriedly. Pam Ovens was my partner that day. After a brief warm-up, I was the first one to serve. After missing the opponent's return shot, I was returning to the service line and I whispered to Pam, "I thought this dress always had double pockets."

She responded, dryly, "It still does, Nelle. Your dress is on *inside out*!"

I was so embarrassed and tickled, but I knew the damage was

already done. "No use to quit now." So I gathered myself together and played until the end of the matches. Afterward, everyone in the foursome and others laughed and laughed. Pam never fails to tease me about it.

Nelle's Memories of the '60s and '70s

When I think back, I was *so blessed* to have been a part of the beginning of Hilton Head. It *was* the chance of a lifetime! Just to be part of a place so beautiful. No one moved to Hilton Head Island with any family's reputation, good or bad. Everyone came because they wanted to live on this gorgeous, lush Island for many reasons—to work hard, to retire, to get a chance to occasionally walk on the long expanse of a sandy beach, to play golf, to fish in the lagoons, to sail a boat, to view the awesome sunrises and sunsets and the colors reflecting on the water, to see the filtered sunlight coming through the dense foliage, and to gaze in awe at the giant live oaks with moss hanging from their limbs.

Every day, one would notice something beautiful not seen before. It was Utopia or Camelot! Because everyone appreciated where we were and worked so hard together so they'd never have to leave this Paradise, it was the happiest place. Those of us who came early are bonded together much like a family. We care about each other deeply, and are always there to help each other.

Now I'm going to tell you what the Island was like in those peaceful, halcyon days. Try to imagine the sound of a wagon on a dirt road moving very slowly. I can hear it creaking along and the courtly black man almost singing, "Ve-ge-*taw*-bles, Ve-ge-*taw*-bles."

Our children would happily exclaim, "It's the Ve-ge-taw-ble Man." The children and I would go out to greet him, and I'd buy fresh vegetables and shrimp or fish. What an awesome experience it was!

Hilton Head was also going to both of the Grant's vegetable stands on Highway 278, which are still there. I always tried to buy something from each of the stands (Mrs. James Grant's and Mrs. Gertrude Grant's), so as not to hurt either one's feelings. In August I always tried to get as many "pigeon peas" as I could buy. They were exceptionally tiny (even smaller than white acre peas), yet so delicious, I wonder if they still grow them.

It was getting stuck in the sand at least once after you moved here. And backing into a palmetto tree, for they were everywhere.

It was almost hitting a deer every time you drove.

It was calling the William Hilton Inn (now the Grand Ocean Marquis Resort) or Roller's Bottle Shop (still on Lagoon Road) to please save some cash out of their daily deposit, if John needed to cash a check to fly to Atlanta or New York for Sea Pines, as *there was no bank*. John or I would usually call Roller's first, as the whiskey store always had more money.

It was showing a film on Sea Pines and having a champagne party every Monday night at the Inn to try to sell property to the few guests. John was usually in charge and never wanted to drink champagne *ever* again.

It was going to a party almost every Saturday night at Charles's house on Green Heron Road in Sea Pines if there were any Inn or rental guests on the Island. John or one of the other three salesmen—Dave Harrell, Herm Seimers, or Wally Butler, or Charles himself—would crack open the sliding glass door so that the curtains would billow out and they could expand on the great ocean breezes. Actually, Charles's small house on Green Heron Road was poorly air-conditioned and often hot. Also, Charles loved to dim the lights if guests stayed too long, which was embarrassing, but the William Hilton Inn stopped serving dinner at 8:30 and male guests were required to dress in "coat and tie" and ladies in appropriate apparel … dresses, no slacks then.

It was playing golf on the Sea Pines Ocean Course, which was the only golf course on the Island then, and maybe not seeing another soul.

It was playing tennis on the one dirt tennis court on the Island, as there was one court only, just outside the original gate to Sea Pines, and kindly waiting your turn.

It was going to the only grocery store on the Island at Coligny Plaza. We bought all our staples there, but had to go to Savannah or Beaufort for most of our fresh meats and other things like broken shoestrings or whatever. Once a week I would put anything needed on my "going to town" list. In the meantime, if I needed a stamp, Mr. Norris Richardson would graciously go into the "post office," which was actually a small cage in the middle of his store, and sell you one. Then he would lock it up and go back to his grocery store needs. There was no post office, except a very small one way down on the northern end of the Island, near Folly Field. The postmistress was Miss Millie, but I didn't go there often as it seemed so far.

It was being sure to have thirty-five cents or a green bridge ticket with you on a trip to Savannah, because that was the toll to get back across the Savannah Talmadge Bridge. A book of sixty tickets could be bought for fifteen dollars, a savings of six dollars.

It was going crabbing at Palmetto Bay Marina and shrimping or fishing in the then brackish water of the lagoons in Sea Pines.

It was going to the William Hilton for the children's swimming lessons in the very modern, kidney-shaped pool. I remember the first lifeguards: Geddes Dowling of Beaufort and Susan Griffin

Woods and Jane Gage Furtado, who both still live on Hilton Head.

It was going to what is now Harbour Town to gather oysters and maybe find our Christmas tree, too.

It was no movie theaters until 1972 (more about that later), and the big treat for a birthday party was to have another mother and me pile the children in the station wagon and go to a movie in Savannah and then go to the Krystal or the Dairy Queen afterward.

It was hurrying to Coligny Circle (near the Laundromat) and trying to beat the McGinty children to the Bookmobile, before they got all the good books. The Bookmobile came for thirty minutes or so every two weeks. There was no library then.

It might be a "Butterfly Day" on Hilton Head in late September or October, when there was a touch of fall in the air. We would take the children in the car and drive down the last dirt road (now the South Beach area) and run to the beach to see if the butterflies were migrating, and, oh yes, if they were and if we sat very still, yellow and monarch butterflies would cover our bodies. I hope they still come. It was an incredible sight.

I will always admire and hold dear the people who had the courage and the vision to move to this paradise of an Island to be a part of creating a community. Looking back, I can understand our parents being worried to death, but we were so young, so poor, and so excited about the opportunity to be a part of something so unique that we weren't afraid at all. (As I tell you about John starting this and my starting that, it's not because we were so great, but we were so fortunate to have this chance and we took it.) John was put in charge of marketing, loved it, and had the vision of ways to "sell" the Island without jeopardizing the beauty of our surroundings. He shared Charles's ideas almost completely. We wanted the best for our children, and if we lacked something we felt we needed, we just started it! There were no rules of previous ways of doing things. There were virtually no parents or grandparents here. You had to make it on your own. This gave all of us in the early days the courage and the freedom to jump in with both feet together.

The scariest part of moving here in 1963 was the lack of doctors. We arrived with a snake bite kit. (Charles warned us not to move here without one.) Yes, that's right, a snake bite kit! John would make me practice where to put the tourniquet, and so on. I prayed I'd never have to use it, and thankfully I didn't. We were told to call the William Hilton Inn to find out if a physician was staying there, and if not, to drive to Beaufort or Savannah right away *after* using the kit. The other essential thing that moved with us was a box of medicine samples from my doctor father with all sorts of instructions. So, a nurse, who was also the Baptist minister's wife, Mrs. Ernest (Sue) Banner, and I dispensed samples when the ailment or injury was nothing serious.

There was no public school on the Island except for the 100 percent black elementary school on the other end of the Island, which was sadly way "behind" the white schools.

John ran for the Beaufort County School Board and was hoping to get a public school for the south end of the Island. (I still have the campaign sheet.) Though he won the election, the public school was denied. In order to keep families with children who were moving to the Island, we had to have a school, but it would have to be a private one instead of public. Charles agreed with John, and as Charles always said after agreeing on an idea, "You've convinced me, John. Now you do it. You take charge." Charles's way of putting the person in charge after convincing him that Sea Pines needed something ensured that whoever came up with the idea would work extremely

The Smith family when John Gettys Smith was running for the Beaufort County School Board.

hard to make it happen. So with that, John became head of the Sea Pines Academy, which later became the Hilton Head Preparatory School.

With the help of the headmaster, Dr. Tom Triol, and a teacher, Mrs. Lillian Goddard, John chose the same curriculum as the highly rated Savannah Country Day School. Then John and Mrs. Goddard, who became the headmistress, hired the teachers. The school began with twenty-nine children in September 1966, in grades one through six. Two of the children were ours, and Ora was still in kindergarten under Mrs. Charlotte Jones. It's hard to believe from this inauspicious beginning, Hilton Head now has many public and private schools. As I remember, Tom Wamsley and Harold Depkin were appointed to be trustees, and they met every Friday, at least, with Mrs. Goddard to discuss plans and problems.

The Sea Pines Academy opened in the old Baptist church building across from the William Hilton Inn. Without asking me, John appointed me to be the first president of the Patrons' Association. When I protested that I hated the PTA and its dull meetings, John said, "Well, you can't ever *not* do it, because there are so few of us, so you might as well do it now. Make the meetings interesting and try to raise a lot of money, too, because the Sea Pines Company is picking up the deficit between tuition and expenses." So I was on, and the job was easy. All the parents came up with ideas to make money, and all the retirees joined in to support the school as well. I continued the Sea Pines Academy Fashion Show and Dance benefit, with my first great cochairman, Jean Corkern, which had been an instant success because everyone on the Island participated. Roller's Bottle Shop always donated the booze, which assured them of their getting the best table. Planter's Hall, in the William Hilton Inn, where the event was held, was happy to have the revenue to more than cover the dinner. The late Jayne Withers trained all the local models, mostly all parents of the schoolchildren. She shocked us ladies before each one walked out on the ramp by saying, "Knockers up!" We gasped, smiled, and did as we were told. I walked out right after Mrs. Maynard Barker (Marianne), and we still laugh about it. Fine's Department Store in Savannah loved the free advertising for their beautiful clothes and gave a 20 percent discount on any outfits that were purchased. John B. Rourke did the same for the men's clothing. The orchestra gave a discount, too, and the Academy made money. There weren't many occasions for a formal affair then. In fact, none that I can recall, so this was the highlight of the winter season.

Then in May we had a May Day affair on the school grounds, which was much like a church bazaar with additions of a May Pole Dance by the children and auctions of paintings led by local auctioneers, that is, my husband John, Bill Cork, Robert Graves, and others. Retirees and

Jayne Withers at the Sea Pines Academy Fashion Show fundraiser.

Nelle Smith at the Sea Pines Academy Fashion Show.

parents donated all sorts of objects for a "White Elephant" or silent auction for wonderful gifts. My favorite Christmas present came from that room. It is a statue hand carved from one piece of wood of the three wise men that Ora Elliott bought for me for Mother's Day for fifty cents, which began as a twelve-dollar item. These two events, the Fashion Show and May Day, became the biggest social events on the Island. Can't wait to show you photos of both events. Oh, I almost forgot to mention three very special happenings in 1964. We were so excited to get a branch of the Bank of Beaufort on our Island. It opened with the funniest hours: from 10 a.m. to noon on Mondays, Wednesdays, and Fridays, and from only 9 to 9:15 a.m. on Tuesdays and Thursdays. (One had to be really quick on those days!) Mr. Eldrid Moody, president of the bank, said the state law required banks to be open five days a week, but it didn't say for how long.

May Pole Dance at Sea Pines Academy.

Groundbreaking ceremony at St. Luke's Episcopal Church.

The famous Captain's Table restaurant in the SeaCrest Motel opened with a gourmet flair. That was exciting.

More importantly in 1964, the Episcopalians had a groundbreaking day for St. Luke's Episcopal Church. I have a picture of that day, a little blurred, but I know everyone in it. In 1965 we had the first service. Prior to that we met at the William Hilton Inn. I was asked to be the superintendent of the Sunday school (a job that lasted over ten years), mainly, I think, because three of the nine children in the Sunday school were Smiths. I taught the first-graders and up, and Dabney Depkin taught the young ones with the help of the late Alice Doughtie.

I have written a history of the first fifty years of Sunday school, but three or four remembrances stand out the most to me, because the now grown-up children always talk about these events.

1. The churning of ice cream on our hand-crank churn to open Sunday school in the fall and when we adjourned in late May. It meant so much to them to "line up for a turn to churn" and to have

ice cream cones afterward. Hard to imagine now, but there was no place on the Island to get an ice cream cone then. I do hope they received some knowledge of the Bible, too.

2. The first Christmas pageant when there were finally enough children in the church for a full cast! We had Mary, Joseph, three shepherds, three wise men, two angels, and two readers. One of the wise men, Thornton Withers, will be forever famous for eating most of the gold coins, chocolate in gold foil, but still the first pageant was a success. This nativity scene's picture was put on the front page of the *Island Packet*, which had just begun its once-a-week publication. We were so proud! Each year following the first pageant was memorable, especially the year one of our young shepherds was crushed, as he was sick and in tears because he didn't feel well enough for his part.

3. The support of the retirees toward the success of our growing Sunday school. Right away I can see Mr. Stafford building the manger scene, another retiree doing the lighting, Mrs. Landon Derby and other ladies beautifying the sanctuary with pine and cedar boughs, Cassina branches with their red berries, magnolia leaves ... all just beautiful. Our organist and choir provided the music. Most of all, I remember the number of retirees whom I persuaded to substitute occasionally for our Sunday school teachers, who were all busy mothers of some of the children. The two who helped to "sub" for me the most were my close neighbor, Mrs. Martha Thompson, the mother of Porter Thompson, and Mrs. Nedra Vandervort, wife of the famed Ben Vandervort, who was portrayed by John Wayne in *The Longest Day*. At that time, I didn't realize he was famous at all. Retirees left their resumes on the other side of the bridge. They built understated homes, all landscape blending as required, and helped every endeavor of our church and our community. One lady who had a great sense of humor, Janet Little, told her maid, "If Nelle

Smith calls, tell her 'No, I won't teach Sunday school.'" We laughed together about that for years!

This Island is so fortunate that the two major developers, Fred Hack and Charles Fraser, were Christians. Fred gave land for all of the churches at the northern end of the Island, and Charles gave all the land for the churches on the southern end of the Island. They realized the importance of including churches within this new Island's infrastructure.

The Holy Family Catholic Church opened its doors in 1973. Joann Capin, told me that four or five years later the priest and congregation realized that more land was needed for parking. However, he was hesitant to ask Charles, because he had already given so much land to them. When he arrived at the Sea Pines office to meet with Charles, the secretary gave the priest the most generous message from Charles. "Give him whatever he wants!"

In 1965, the Island's first physician, Dr. Chet Goddard, opened his practice. Dr. Bill Fries came to assist him in 1966. Our first dentist was the late Dr. Joseph List, who moved here with his wife, Dottie, and children, Michael, Michelle, and Patrick. They became very involved with the school and the church, and became good friends of our children.

That same year, we moved into our new house, which was designed by McGinty and Stanley and built by Farris Highsmith for $37,500—a beautiful thirty-three-hundred-square-foot home. Imagine that now! We were scared to sign the mortgage loan because the payments of $245 a month seemed like a great deal of money.

Also in 1965, Mrs. Em Palmer, wife of Wallace (Wally), our head pro at Sea Pines, and Mrs. Edith Boyd, wife of Clyde, our assistant pro, began the first Cub Scout troop on Hilton Head. We felt the need for this organization for our boys and finally found eight boys scattered over the Island who were eight years old. The school bus from Bluff-ton let them get off twice a week at St. Luke's, which allowed us to use their Sunday school room. We tried to teach them sports, beginning with softball. It was a disaster, because most of them cried when we'd call "Out!" We soon realized that since there were virtually no neigh-borhoods, these little boys had never seen the game played by older kids and didn't know how the older boys would've acted. Moreover, the Island could only receive three TV stations, and no little boys or older children stayed inside then, with all this natural space around them. They built forts, fished, crabbed, and explored.

Our scariest experience was being chased by wild boars—I think—during a hike in the woods. When I heard those thundering hoof-steps behind us, I yelled, "Run for your lives, boys. Back to the church!" Thankfully, they ran like crazy, and no one was hurt.

Living on the Island in those days was going to the beach every day if you wanted to. Occasionally, there would be horses or even cars on the beach, and for a number of years there were no leashed dogs on the sand, either.

The Smith house at 9 Beach Lagoon Road.

Close up of the front door at 9 Beach Lagoon Road.

I learned quickly that anyone who worked for Sea Pines was literally on call 24/7! Charles was an intense genius, and if something was on his mind, he'd come to our house no matter how late. He once arrived at 11:30 p.m., saying, "I know it's late, but your light was still on in your bedroom, so I knew you were awake." No one *locked* their doors *then*, so Charles just walked inside, talking loudly and enthusiastically. John was expected and did get ready to hear his latest idea or ideas and to give a well-thought-out opinion, no matter what time it was. John's parents, who were visiting that night, were shocked at Charles's late arrival.

Sundays after church were not days of rest either. We learned to rush home from church, saying, "Let's see who can get your bathing suits on the fastest and head for the beach." Charles caught on to that and would find us, no matter how many times we'd change our places on the wide expanse of beach. He would come with an arm full of papers that would blow everywhere.

John was quoted by Furman Bisher as saying, "We don't relax on this Island. We live on the run so that others may relax." That was certainly true for anyone who worked for Sea Pines.

You may have heard that Charles could be rude. Well, that's the truth, he could be. Many times when invited to a party with important guests in attendance, he would sit down with one of the hosts' magazines and pore over an article and even tear the page or pages out. He would be completely engrossed in his reading and completely oblivious to those around him. Many feelings were hurt at being ignored, the guests as well as his staff. His behavior could be very frustrating and irritating. Deep down, though, Charles was kind and generous, but that "not being aware of people's feelings" was his Achilles heel with many people. Some never forgave him.

The Plantation Club opened in May 1966 with a grand affair.

All members had to sign in with their member numbers. John was number three, after Joe Fraser. Charles was naturally number one.

I remember being so excited over deciding what to wear. All the ladies were, I'm sure. I was so excited to find a formal at Fine's Department Store in Savannah that had the most popular "hot pants" under it. Our outstanding county photographer, Mr. Ned Brown of Beaufort, took a picture of John and me at that affair. He took almost all the special-occasion pictures for years. John called him to come over all the time, and we became such good friends.

John was the overall executive in charge of the Club for many years. For lots of us, the fun began months before at "tasting parties" with Chef Franz Meier in charge of all the food, with suggestions from all of us with our favorite recipes. We got to vote on favorite entrees. I remember being so glad that Meeting Street Crab Casserole won as one to be served. Who can forget the Beef Steak Clarendon, the Shad Roe, the Hearts of Palm Salad, or the Caesar Salad made at the table by a waiter rubbing the interior of a wooden salad bowl with a garlic clove—this was definitely first class—and ending with Bananas Foster or Cherries Jubilee Flambé!

It was the Lowcountry's first experience with European services, with thick German accents everywhere. One waiter, named Hanz, was so handsome that it was rumored ladies left their room keys on the table or in their chairs. Dining at the Plantation Club was especially fun for me, as prior to the Club opening all the entertaining was previously at our house. There was no caterer on the Island then, and part of John's job was to entertain writers who might write a story about Sea Pines or the Island. There were many quick clean-ups of the house by me and the children, and my making dips, cheese straws, and the new anchovy puffs, which are still some of my favorite things to make for a party for hors d'oeuvres.

Part of the William Hilton Inn, Planter's Hall, also opened in August 1966. This space was needed for many purposes. Its folding doors could make the large space great for small or large conventions, there was a stage for plays, and it was a perfect place for a dance or a large banquet.

For some time, John had planned a South Carolina Homecoming for native South Carolinians who had achieved success and fame—military brass such as General William Westmoreland, noted CBS broadcaster Frank Blair from Yemassee, and many others who were listed in Who's Who. I remember well his going through those lists and getting excited if the person was born in South Carolina. Now with Planter's Hall and the Plantation Club opening in 1966, the invited guest could be royally entertained.

During November 18–22, 1966, the native South Carolinians were invited to a South Carolina homecoming complete with golf, a tour of homes, elegant to-dos, and casual parties. This weekend was quite a success. Many of the guests bought property and helped spread the word about this idyllic place. John Simpson, vice president of Westinghouse, and his wife, built a beachfront home right across from the Lagoon bridge adjacent to our house. They became good friends and neighbors.

All of the retirees on our street welcomed trick–or–treaters, including our three, all the Doughties' children, the McGintys, the Withers, and the Craigheads. Our children loved to visit the Ralph Ballantines because his wife, Sis, dressed up like a witch and even told fortunes. One of the neighbors, I think it was General Timberlake, gave each of the children a roll of nickels, which was much better than an apple that one or two of the retirees gave.

In 1967 Arnold Palmer first came to Hilton Head. In fact, he "saved the day for Bruce Devlin," who was then the Sea Pines Golf Touring

Pro. Due to a mistake by Bruce's manager on the very day the celebrity was expected, John got the word that he was not coming. The "big press day" was already planned adjacent to the Sea Pines Pro Shop, and Bruce was to demonstrate ways to improve your golf strokes and putting. I remember it well as John was in charge. Arnie heard of the dilemma and said he'd be glad to come and sub for Bruce. What a sub he turned out to be. This was before the 1969 Heritage. Arnie's plane landed on our newly paved thirty-seven-hundred-foot-long airstrip. No jet had ever landed there before. Arnie was so impressed by the beauty of the Island that he bought an oceanfront lot that very day.

One of my favorite Sea Pines stories is an Island joke. One Tuesday, I was driving the carpool to Savannah Country Day and the Catholic school, as Sea Pines Academy just had six grades until fall of 1976 when the high school was opened. After leaving the children at their schools, I went by Arnstein's Dry Cleaning to pick up my cleaning. This dry cleaner was known as *the* place to take a formal. My dress was not ready, and I needed it desperately because I was flying to New York with John the next day for a special Sea Pines black-tie business affair. I *had* to have that long dress. Mr. Arnstein felt so bad that the dress wouldn't be ready until 5 p.m. He knew I couldn't wait that long. I had to pick up the children at 3 p.m. and get them back home to the Island. He said, "Mrs. Smith, is there anyone else from Hilton Head here today or anyone you know coming to the Island who could bring it to you?"

I thought quickly of our dinner guests who were in Savannah that day, and meeting us at the Plantation Club that night were none other than Burt Reynolds and his stunt man. They were coming to Hilton Head that night to shoot a scene for a movie the next day. But did I dare ask him to bring my dry cleaning? I had no choice. I asked Mr. Arnstein to deliver the dress to the DeSoto Hotel for me and that, of course, I would pay him extra for that. He said, "Oh no, you won't pay me, it's my fault!" He nearly fell over when I wrote a note to Burt Reynolds (whom, of course, I had never met) and asked him if he would be so kind as to bring my dry cleaning to the Plantation Club. Burt was so cute about it later, saying, "Delivering dry cleaning was a first for me!" I was worried because Arnstein's put all their formals on a very sexy cardboard mannequin. I nearly died from embarrassment when Burt took the mannequin out of his trunk. But it made our evening begin with much laughing, and we all had the most fun evening! (I wonder if Burt even remembers it? Probably not, but I do.)

Of course, the sports attractions, namely the Heritage golf and Family Circle tennis tournaments, put Hilton Head in the limelight, but they didn't come without incredible work, risk, and luck. For six years, John had been courting magazine editors, but it was difficult as they had never heard of Sea Pines Plantation or Hilton Head Island and were pretty vague about South Carolina. The first question always was, "Now, where is this Island?" As John felt that a major golf tournament would eventually do the trick. He and Charles, of course, and others planned the third course, Harbour Town, just for a tournament, mainly because they financially could not afford to close the other courses for it. John felt the time was right, though neither the Yacht Basin nor the Lighthouse was yet completed, as you see in the pictures.

The company was desperate for money, too. It seems to me that we were always desperately hoping for a loan from Traveler's Insurance to even receive paychecks then! Charles became convinced that it could and should be done and be successful. Consequently, he said, "All right, John, go do it!"

So John became the tournament's chairman at that moment for the next five years. He named it the Heritage, in honor of the game's origin in Scotland. The Scots brought the game to Charleston and founded the South Carolina Golf Association, which is the oldest golf club in America. John designed the plaid, altering the Royal Stewart plaid, and had cloth woven for the winning jacket and the hostess scarves. Thanksgiving was chosen as the date for the tournament as the time was open on the PGA schedule and it was a family time. Golfers brought their families, and John asked many of the Sea Pines residents to host them. Golfers didn't have any money to spend on lodging, and the residents loved having a pro and his family stay with them. Magazine writers came with their families because of the "comp" rooms and some of them as a gesture of friendship to John. All of them were invited to shrimp boils, a cocktail buffet party at our house, and they especially loved the oyster roast at the Donald O'Quinns' house and garden. All Islanders, not just Sea Pines residents, were involved and volunteered to help the tournament. School was let out. All the older kids carried banners, washed golf balls, and did anything else needed. Our son Gettys, twelve, began with friends like King Merritt, Reb and Bill Thomas. But Spencer at ten years old was the most excited because he was on the Academy Junior Golf team and was in "hog heaven" following the golfers around the course. Even Ora Elliott, age eight, was thrilled to have her picture taken with Jack Nicklaus, who designed the course, along with Pete Dye.

There are so many stories about the Heritage, and my favorite is the same as John's: The most joyous moment when Arnie's putt dropped into the hole for a winner. I was so proud of John and everyone on the Island. Islanders were blessed with an optimistic spirit in those early years and a "can-do-anything-togetherness" that accomplished so much.

The Heritage wasn't televised until 1974, when the tournament was

*Jack Nicklaus with Ora Smith, Michele Merritt with Diane and
Paige Mallard at the first Heritage Golf Tournament.*

changed to the spring, but what a momentous beginning we had. What an impact that tournament has had on us, the county, and the state!

You will notice that the tournament logo changed from the Compass Rose to the Harbour Town Lighthouse (after Sea Pines) with the television exposure, as John always asked that they begin and end the filming with the Lighthouse. I remember John teasing Charles that the tournament needed a symbol, something that would be instantly recognized, like the Eiffel Tower in Paris. He said that soon Sea Pines' logo would be the Harbour Town Lighthouse, not the Compass Rose. Charles would go up on his toes, laugh, and protest, saying, "Never!" But he loved the idea that it would and loved the bantering of ideas.

John and I always had a big party for the players and many Islanders on Thursday night of the tennis tournaments at Turtle Lane Cabanas, but he left out what happened afterward. Ha! John usually asked everyone to come on over to our house for breakfast and more dancing on our terrazzo floors. I can still see Jane Withers dancing with Roy Emerson. We cooked bacon, scrambled a million eggs, and were in and out of the kitchen fixing breakfast. After everyone left, our house was often a disastrous mess, but we—all of us—got to really know the players and dance with them. Oh, what fun we had, especially with the Aussies!

Something happened in the fall of 1969 that could have ruined all of the waters in Beaufort County and beyond. A German company, BASF, announced plans to build a petrochemical plant on Victoria Bluff, near Bluffton. Rumors had been flying around that this was happening, but seeing the headlines was so frightening. John, Charles, Fred Hack, and especially his younger brother, Orion Hack, and many others united with the black fishing cooperative to work together to not allow this to happen. Schoolchildren got involved, too, by making posters reading, "Bad Air!" "Sick Fish!" "Don't Pollute!" Petitions against its coming here were signed all over Hilton Head. Children wrote Secretary of the Interior Hickel letters begging him to use his influence against BASF. Most blacks and whites were united because fishing, shrimping, and oystering were their way of life. Some blacks were for the plant coming because higher-paying jobs were promised. Beaufort County and our state were very poor then, and much of northern Beaufort County lobbied for the plant. Good friends of many of ours disagreed with us and fought against it. It caused a lot of hard feelings. I remember Helen Harvey, who was one of my roommates at Carolina, calling me and saying, "Nelle, I can't believe that John is against BASF, against *progress*. They say they won't pollute!"

I exclaimed, "Oh, Helen, it'll be too late if they do pollute. I'm just as sad that Brantley's law firm is representing the plant. I've seen what they did to the Rhine River. There's no way the company can possibly promise 100 percent that it will not pollute. BASF has already polluted an area in Texas—or is it Louisiana? —that's now known as Cancer Alley! The resort industry on Hilton Head and the golf courses will bring business for the area. Pollution will change the Lowcountry, not just Hilton Head and Bluffton, but Beaufort will be affected, too." We decided, then and there, not to let this ruin our friendship, but both couples had to work at it. To this day, thankfully, we're still good friends.

David Lauderdale's column in the *Island Packet*, December 18, 2016, is a most accurate account of the turbulent two years in our county and state. Protecting the environment was not widespread then, before Rachel Carson's *Silent Spring*, but ecology was beginning. There were definitely oil spills in rivers.

The publicity brought by Arnie Palmer winning the Heritage in November of that same year, 1969, surely helped to show that Hilton Head was especially beautiful and would have a positive impact on our county and state. However, I feel that the shrimp boat *Capt. Dave I*'s trip to Washington via water to deliver over thirty-five thousand signatures to not allow BASF to come to Victoria Bluff was the turning point toward conserving our waters. I'll never forget the planning of that trip: for three whites and three blacks to go up the Waterway, sleeping and eating on the boat for eight to ten days, gathering more signatures at each stop, reportedly forty thousand or more as the total count. signatures to hand deliver to Interior Secretary Hickel. I knew every man on that boat. John promoted this trip passionately, and when their families wished them bon voyage from Skull Creek, I was a little worried. There were no cell phones then. Ora Elliott, eight years old, was worried that she would never see her daddy again!

Not only was the trip successful, but John said the food on that boat was the best he'd ever eaten. The "Cruise for Conservation" got much coverage from the media. All of us welcomed the boat and crew home at Harbour Town, when Harbour Town was just beginning; the lighthouse wasn't finished, nor all the shops. Secretary Hickel wrote the head of BASF to present proof that they would not pollute. Fortunately, the company executives decided to put their plans of building a petrochemical plant on hold. But this fight of BASF possibly coming to Victoria Bluff was not really over until two years later, in January 1971. We were all so relieved. Just think of the valiant people who stood up for our beautiful Lowcountry and its pristine waters. The children in school wrote thank-you letters to Secretary Hickel, and he wrote back to each child! I still have Ora Elliott's letter and his response. I'm so glad I saved them.

Signed petitions delivered to Secretary of the Interior, Walter J. Hickel.

Walter J. Hickel

907-279-9401
935 THIRD AVENUE
ANCHORAGE, ALASKA 99501

February 22, 1972

Ora Elliott
Sea Pines Academy
Hilton Head Island
South Carolina 29928

Dear Ora:

My thanks for the outstanding letter which
you sent to me when Mrs. Hickel and I visited
Hilton Head.

You mentioned that you have lived on the island
for eight years, so you certainly know a great
deal more of its beauty than I. However, in just
the short time I was there I could see that the
effort to protect your environment was well worth
it.

Keep up the good work.

Sincerely,

Walter J. Hickel

Walter J. Hickel letter.

79

Executive Travels

Often in January, Charles treated the executives and their wives to a weeklong trip, to brainstorm and explore other new Island resorts in the warm Caribbean. One resort actually ran out of food, but the Island natives saved our lives by bringing fresh seafood to the chef, plus fruits and vegetables.

One of the wives recalls there were no screens on the windows of the rooms, and a mouse came and jumped into her suitcase. Quickly, she snapped the suitcase shut and then ran outside to let the mouse out! She prayed it wouldn't come back.

The William Holmes Family

One of the best native Islander families came into our lives in 1965. At the time, I was desperately trying to be a good wife to John and to be an asset to John's business by entertaining guests at our home or taking them out for dinner. At the same time, I was torn between being a good mother to our children, just eight, six, and four—and having to go out at night so much. I tried out many nice babysitters, but I realized the children needed more consistency in their lives. Each new person was a new adjustment for them.

I knew immediately that I had found the perfect person when a sixteen-year-old black girl, Lauretta Holmes, came to babysit for us. She fit like a glove and had the nicest manners. After a few weeks or more, I talked to Lauretta and her mother about Lauretta being "on call" as many nights as was needed, as long as it didn't interfere with her schoolwork.

Mr. and Mrs. Holmes worked for the Gerhards down the street from us in Sea Pines. They left work after cooking and serving dinner at night. They usually drove back to their home off Gumtree Road between 8:30 and 9:30 p.m. Often John would take Lauretta to the Gerhards in time for her to ride home with them, which helped John a great deal, because Highway 278 was a dark, lonely road *then*.

Also, we had a small room upstairs, like a den, with a sofa bed and a television. It was adjacent to the boys' bedroom and bathroom. Occasionally, Lauretta got off the school bus with her books and would do her homework, spend the night, and then ride the school bus back to high school the next day. She kept extra clothes at our house. She became much like an older sister to the children, and a second daughter to us.

She could keep order, too. John told Lauretta to call us if the children were misbehaving or out of control. One night, Lauretta called us at General and Mrs. Timberlake's house, where we were for a neighborhood party (nicknamed by all as a "six-to-eighter" party—arrive at six and leave at eight.)

I was in the dining room with guests gathered around, sampling hors d'oeuvres. I was wondering why John hadn't followed me because I knew the food would be so good and would be our supper or dinner. Thinking John was just still talking to the other guests in the living room, I wasn't concerned. When he finally came into the dining room, I greeted him saying, "Where have you been? This food is delicious."

John answered, "I have just been home to *spank* all three of *your* children!"

I exclaimed, "Oh, no, what in the world were they doing?"

He said, "They were throwing food at each other." (a 'food fight')".

Needless to say, Lauretta never had to call either one of us again.

In 1967 a Canadian editor and publisher, a business friend of John's, offered his house in Montreal free of charge for a week's stay. The house was directly across from Expo '67! We were thrilled at that opportunity. John excitedly said, "Nelle, let's ask Lauretta to go with us to help with the children, and then just the two of us can go out at night sometimes. Also, let's spend a few days in Washington and New York. It will be such an education for the kids and Lauretta, too."

I talked it over with Lauretta, and she was thrilled over flying, going to New York, Washington, and Expo '67. I knew I had to convince Mr. and Mrs. Holmes first, though.

I will never forget that visit with Mrs. Holmes. She listened very carefully to everything I said. I told her that Lauretta would be our guest, of course, and that in addition, we would pay her for any time she looked after the children at night. She asked me only one question, saying, "Mrs. Smith, are you trying to take my baby girl *away* from me?"

I answered, "Oh, no, Mrs. Holmes. I would never do that. I just want to enrich her life." She smiled sweetly and we just stood and hugged each other in agreement. We had one of the best times ever as a family on that trip!

Lauretta saved money from babysitting and graduated from Benedict College in Columbia. Her sister, Annie Lou, took Lauretta's place while she was away at college. We love her so much, too. Lauretta would often surprise us early on Saturday mornings when she came home for the weekend. We'd hear bacon frying and dishes being taken out of the dishwasher, and one of the children would scream, "Lauretta's home!"

Now I'm so blessed to be in the same town, Beaufort, near Lauretta and her husband, Patrick Young. We keep in touch with them with telephone calls, cards, and visits celebrating weddings, graduations, and even funerals. Lauretta has always been a tremendous support during our sad times with her loving presence. There are no words to adequately describe the depth of my feelings and gratitude to this outstanding Holmes Family.

Perhaps an article about this family by Carolyn Grant, about Mr. William Holmes, describes them best. This was published in the *Island Packet* and well worth reading.

"Manners Take You Places That Money Can't!"

A return to manners is a return to the old ways of Hilton Head

. A wise old islander, Mr. William Holmes Sr., once told me his key to survival on Hilton Head Island was practicing what his mother taught him: manners.

"Manners will take you where money can't," he told me one day in a conversation about his life. I always remember this piece of advice because it is a very true statement. The lack of manners can indeed be a turn-off.

My thoughts on manners are triggered by Gov. Jim Hodges' push for legislation on value education that would teach students to say "yes, ma'am; no, ma'am," and other kind responses to figures of authority, and to show courtesy.

It's sad that manners have to be legislated. It's sad that somehow through the generations respectful responses

and other basic manners were lost in the upbringing of children. Yet manners, as Mr. Holmes and other wise elders would tell children, will take you even further than being in

CAROLYN GRANT

your best suit at an interview or earning a place on the honor roll.

Mr. Holmes, now 84 and living in a nursing facility, was born and reared on Hilton Head before the world even knew it existed. Yet the people living on it — many of them dirt poor — had manners. What they lacked financially, they made up for in character.

Your manners — saying "yes, ma'am," "no, sir," "thank you" and "please" — were just as common as breathing. You couldn't get along without them. Manners were easily taught. What were laid down as rules and values at home were stressed earnestly in school and in the community. You addressed your elders, figures of authority and relatives with the proper titles, not by calling them by their first names.

If you behaved otherwise, you were disciplined (the rod was not spared) at school and at home. Your manners reflected the kind of home training you received. In Hilton Head's pre-development era, good manners were your ticket off this island devoid of jobs, postelementary education and a viable economic market.

Islanders migrated to Boston, New York, Philadelphia, Miami, Savannah, Beaufort and St. Helena Island for jobs and boarding school. They left with more manners than money, and had to live with relatives who extended hospitality for long periods of time. Little was expected in return other than good, sensible manners and respect for your host family. In time, you would repay your relative or host with a little money, favors and acts of kindness.

Etched forever in your mind would be the kindness they shared as you struggled to work and get a place of your own, make a decent living or finish your education.

At the cornerstone of success for many people today are the manners they gained in their youth that never disappeared from their daily lives.

By legislating manners, we run the

risk of some students rebelling simply because they're being made to respond with certain statements at school or with responses they rarely use in their daily lives.

At least one opponent of legislation on manners and values feels requiring students to say "yes, ma'am" and other courteous remarks would be a throwback to slavery and would send the wrong message to children, especially black children. In days of slavery, you were whipped if you didn't give the proper response to slave owners or overseers.

The issue of slavery and what happened in that era is another matter. What I do know is that showing manners and respect were taught and learned as a part of one's upbringing, during and after slavery.

I hope that we would make manners

more of a natural part of our lives and realize they are virtues that should be extended in our everyday lives. Teaching manners and values should begin at home, and respectful behavior should be encouraged to take place at school and in other settings.

One of the most important lessons that should be stressed in all environments is the one Mr. Holmes and others learned as they survived on a barren island — that when your pocket is empty, what you carry in your heart will pay your way. And even if you have some possession to give, it's still best to give it respectfully.

This is a lesson you can carry with you to school and to work, and one that will help you be successful in life each day.

Carolyn Grant is a native Hilton Head Islander and a free-lance writer.

A return to manners is a return to the old ways of Hilton Head.

Nell's Harbour Shop

Something very important happened to me in 1971. I began my most successful career: Nell's Harbour Shop, which is now the oldest gift shop still in business on the Island.

Now I'm going to tell you exactly how it all began. (I shared this history with the Clover Club, a ladies' club in Beaufort, on January 23, 2012.)

Nelle Smith in front of Nell's Harbour Shop.

My Most Successful Career, or Twenty-Five Years of Owning Nell's Harbour Shop

Presented to the Clover Club by Nelle M. Smith

MONDAY, JANUARY 23, 2012

One afternoon in early 1970, John returned home late from working all day with Charles Fraser on the construction of the Harbour Town shops, which were under construction. He walked in with a quick in his step and enthusiastically announced, "Guess what, Nelle? I've just signed an option for the number-one spot at Harbour Town for a shop for us!" It was the word "us" that panicked me. Most of you will remember that we had run a restaurant "just on the weekends" to save Brattonsville, while we both had full-time jobs teaching and working for a newspaper during the week, and at the same time were raising two babies: Gettys, two, and Spencer, four months old. No wonder I was fearful!

So I took a deep breath and said, "Oh, John, that's just wonderful, but I want it in *writing* that I have nothing to do with that shop, absolutely nothing. I don't want to be involved at all."

He said something like, "Oh, Nelle, don't worry! I'm not thinking of your running the shop. I'm getting someone with experience who has managed a successful business. I'm planning on running an ad in the *Wall Street Journal*. But you may want to work there for a day or two when the children get older."

86

Well, I *fell* for what he said again. There was no signing of any paper, and John advertised in the *Wall Street Journal*, interviewed and hired a lady who seemed perfect, Mrs. Frances Morton. She and her husband had run the well-known Andrew Morton gift shop in Knoxville, but they were getting a divorce.

Our silent partner, Mr. Joe Elvove, who turned out to be anything but silent, agreed Frances would give the shop a great beginning, which she did. However, Joe was vice president of Dixie Crystal Sugar Company in Savannah, and he had big ideas of the office equipment and things needed for this small new shop. He installed a huge Xerox machine that took up half the office. Only the Sea Pines Company had a Xerox machine on the Island then, and theirs was smaller than ours.

Joe also bought a large, complicated cash register that needed a guidebook to operate. He demanded that we rent a large warehouse space, and there was not enough surplus merchandise to store in it.

In addition, Joe decided that one part of the shop should sell nautical antiques, shipped from London, which proved to be a costly disaster. We received antique barometers, a decorative figurehead, sextants, small cannons, a ship's wheel, brass bells, portholes, telescopes, clocks, and more. These were all expensive and difficult to sell to the few tourists and Islanders. I realize now that Joe's ideas and demands were unintentional mistakes, because he was vice president of a huge business in a city, and this was a small 1,305-square-foot space on a sparsely inhabited Island.

Nevertheless, our shop, first called the Hilton Head Harbour Shop, opened on August 15, 1971, with much enthusiasm but few people. Harbour Town was very new and very quiet. There were only a dozen or so villas all the way from Harbour Town to the old Plantation Club. It's hard to believe now.

After a few slow months and poor cash flow, trouble really mushroomed between Frances and our partner, Joe.

When John left town on business, she would call me and cry, and Joe would call and curse Frances and her abilities. He wanted to sue her for criminal negligence. It was awful. We refused to sue, knowing that she was just going through a sad divorce, and the woes of beginning a new business. She wanted to quit and move, and Joe just wanted to close the shop and halve the losses. John, fortunately *now*, felt the potential was too great to do that. He said, "Nelle, please let's take it over ourselves with all the losses. If you'll just work for two weeks, I'll find us another manager—just two weeks. We must not give up this space. Sea Pines and this Island are on the verge of being known everywhere."

So, of course, I said, "Well, yes, I'll do it, but *just* for two weeks." I wasn't nearly as afraid as I should have been.

At the time, though, and I'll set the stage for you, there was an optimism that was contagious on the Island. We were all young, new, had moved from many different places with no blueprint of how things were begun, and no good family reputation on which to lean. Everyone had to make it on his own, and most felt we could accomplish anything if we worked hard enough. After all, we had all worked together for the first Heritage in November of 1969 and Arnold Palmer had won. The Island was Utopia which became Camelot for many years, but it took a while.

Back to my first two weeks, I jumped in never having taken a business or bookkeeping course, not even typing. My mother always required us to take Bible in high school all four years when I had an elective because the Presbyterian church helped support the Bible teacher and that was that! Years later, I would tease her, "Momma, don't you wish you had let me take at least one business course. Just think how much more successful I would have been." She would answer firmly, "Those Bible courses never hurt you, Nelle."

I realized in *much* less than two weeks that we couldn't hire a manager for sure, and couldn't even pay me, as we owed seventy thousand dollars, which would be like seven hundred thousand dollars now. We were in a bad situation financially.

I began by writing a letter to each vendor we owed that we were the new managers—were good, honest people, would definitely pay them back, but that it would have to be terribly slow: just a few dollars each month, and to please not charge us interest but that our word was good. Every company responded to us, and none charged us interest. Imagine that now?

I knew immediately to cancel our lease with the Xerox machine, which was costing $180 a month. Next I sold the cash register to Signe Gardo for her new bakery that had just opened. In less than a week, she called and pleaded, "Nelle, would you possibly let me return this cash register? It's just awful."

I laughed and said, "Oh no, Signe, I don't want it back. Just sell it to someone else. You can do it." We were using a box for our cash and hand writing our tickets, which was all we needed then. Signe kept that cash register for years and years, and I never failed to tease her about it.

Next I canceled our warehouse space, sold my car, and bought a van (with no name on it, of course, as Sea Pines would have never allowed that to be parked in my yard) in which to keep extra stock. I paid Gettys and a friend to put up shelves in our garden and tool house, which became our inexpensive warehouse! Of course, no shipments were sent to our house. Everything was shipped to Harbour Town.

Sometimes extra stock overflowed to under all of our beds at home, too. Some things fit just right under the beds: boxed luggage racks, boxed Pawley's Island hammocks, framed prints of West Fraser and Ray Ellis, and other things all fit perfectly. If a customer needed something that was at home, we'd just say, "Just give us fifteen or twenty minutes and we'll go get it from our warehouse." It worked like a charm. It was hard work, too, loading extra stock in the van, then unloading at our house or warehouse, but we saved a great deal of money.

Time came for us to attend our first gift show in New York, which is hilarious now. I took an alphabetized list of whom we owed with me.

When we'd see a beautiful showroom, John would say, "Oh, let's go in here. I see some great things." I'd check my list first, though, and frequently say, "Oh no, John, we can't go in there. We owe them. We'll have to find another company that sells similar things." John was great at choosing pretty, expensive, and unique things, and I was the practical one—a good blend, I guess. It took me an hour to complete my first order, which had a one-hundred-dollar minimum to open, and I was so slow. It was with Woodchips Designs for nautical potholders and kitchen towels. To make matters worse, I called back to our shop and my employee had not seen a customer all day and it was one o'clock. I begged *her* to buy something, that I'd pay her back, as I didn't want a day of no sales. It was very slow then.

I made so many mistakes and there are so many funny stories that I've struggled as to which stories to share—some I can't tell. Should I tell you about my writing and mailing ten thousand dollars worth of checks out of the wrong bank account? By mistake, the Bank of Savannah, from whom we had borrowed money, had sent me new checks with the same color as my other Bank of Beaufort checking account. That threw me. I had to call Larry Dunn, a good friend, husband of the successful Realtor Celia Dunn, and had to beg him not to bounce the checks or charge me overdrafts! He still teases me about that every time I see them and asks, "Written any checks lately, Nelle?"

Or should I tell you about the frantic man barging his way into the shop in front of three or four customers, when we were so busy, with something in his clinched hand and demanded, "Do you sell this?"

I said, "But, sir, what is it?" I was trying to kill him with kindness.

He opened his hand and said, "It's a battery for my hearing aid!"

I said, "No, I'm sorry, but we don't sell batteries."

He angrily said, "Well, what do you people *do* on this Island, go *deaf*?"

I answered calmly, "No, sir, we go to Savannah."

He stalked out and everyone laughed. He came back later and apologized, and I offered to get him a battery the next day, because I was driving the Tuesday carpool to Savannah Country Day.

Now I'm going to tell you about some of our successes. John and I were walking the aisles of the temporary booths at the Atlanta Gift Show hoping to find something new. That is almost as necessary to keep one's competitive edge, as restocking the proven sellers. We passed this booth with these ugly dolls, some dressed as boys, some as girls, in a playpen. The ugliest one of all was a bald baby boy named "Otis Lee." I'll never forget him in a high chair. He had a big sign around his neck saying, "Please adopt me; I need a home." John hurried on down the aisle saying, "Nelle, don't even slow down, no one will buy those ugly dolls, no one!" I hurried after him saying, "Stop, John, look back at all the women hugging those dolls." Oh, what a successful run for years we had with the "Little People," which became the Cabbage Patch Kids. One in a baseball outfit was named Charles Spencer McCants, which I gave to my daddy for the boy he had always wanted. The next year I gave him a little friend or pal (preemie) as Charles Spencer was so lonely. That's the way we talked—that was the make-believe world of those dolls. For a long time, I was the only "adoptable" shop in the state.

I am going to pass a picture of me in a nurse's uniform, borrowed from Mrs. Linda Laughlin, which I dressed up in for our annual Valentine Tea Party. I'd serve pink lemonade, pink cupcakes, and all the mothers and babies would have the best time. People came from everywhere.

Probably the best-income producing decision I ever made was when a young friend, now Mrs. Laura Kolb, came in seeking help in choosing china, crystal, and so on for her upcoming wedding. I decided to go ahead and open the first bridal registry on the Island. Our shop was perfect for this, as we already carried almost all the accessories that a couple needed. I talked companies into shipping us a place setting of the chosen china and crystal patterns. There was no mall on the Island, no outlets, no Bed Bath and Beyond. We were the only bridal registry for a number of years. This increased our business and customer base tremendously. The couples, especially the brides, became our friends and loyal customers.

Friends and customers also helped us by suggesting items that we should sell. We listened to them and wrote their advice and desires in a notebook. One customer called and asked about a new game called Trivial Pursuit. We looked into it and sold so many of those games before everyone knew about them.

One Christmas I received a box of the most delicious chocolates, all nautical shaped candy: sailboats or sloops, sand dollars, and scallop shells, which seemed to be made for Harbour Town. We immediately ordered these to add to our thriving gourmet section. We did so well that the owners chose our shop as one of three in the country to be featured in their national advertising campaign, such as in *Town and Country* magazine, with a heading saying, "Sweet Sloops, simply the best chocolates in the world, seen at shops such as Cooleys Marco Polo of Boston, Mildred Hoit of Palm Beach, and Nell's Harbour Shop of Hilton Head." We were so proud.

Business was so good and fun in the next few years. The Heritage was so successful in the spring. One year after Nick Faldo had just won the Masters, he ordered one of our "rocking boats." Nell's sold a "rocking boat" instead of a rocking horse, for his new baby boy. Nell's still takes orders from the sample boat, which is always in front of the shop. He named his boat the "S.S. *Faldo*." That was so special getting to know the golfers and their wives, and then came the Family Circle Cup with all the tennis players and their families. In addition, Gregg Russell sang every night in front of our shop during the season. We definitely had the best location.

All the college students wanted to come to the Island in the summer to work, including nieces, nephews, and cousins, which was great. Some even lived with us. Our children loved it, and our boys couldn't wait to check out the new girls hired each summer.

One day I received a resume from Ora, who had been working in Columbia, and knew one of my full-time employees was moving away. It was risky, mother and daughter working together, but we agreed to try it for a year. She turned out to be the best addition ever. We had some adjusting to do, but we became great friends, good coworkers, and continue to love each other, too.

One innovative thing we did to help our employees remember how to do things, and particularly to help new employees, was to develop a reference manual from all our notes throughout the years. It contains sections such as "How to Treat a Customer," "How to Sell," "How to Run the Cash Register," "How to Register a Bride," and so on. We jokingly named it "The Book of Life."

From 1985 on for a couple of years, the Island and especially

Harbour Town fell on hard times. Interest rates skyrocketed, and Charles Fraser had to sell parts of Harbour Town. First came the bumper sticker "Honk if Bobby owes YOU," referring to Bobby Ginn of Hampton, South Carolina, whose failed company had bought almost all of Harbour Town. Then new companies bought part of Harbour Town and Sea Pines. Does anyone remember Luke Taylor and his partners, that owned a company called the Cuyahoga Wrecking Company? The Calibogue Café, now the Crazy Crab, had a Grand Opening one night and closed the next day. The Racquet Club and Pro Shop closed. The tennis nets were taken down. Even the water fountains were removed, and golf ball suppliers refused to ship to the Heritage golf shop, unless they got paid in advance.

During this time, several shops, including ours, were operating on a month-to-month lease. We had to continue paying rent, ordering stock, not knowing if we'd be thrown out or not, with no place to go. That happened to the shop next door to us, Shoes Etc., owned by the Marchettis, which was a great shop.

We had been considering opening a second shop anyway, to better serve existing customers who did not live in Sea Pines. The Island was exploding in growth, and some people resented the gate fee. With no lease now, it was imperative to open a second shop, if at all possible.

Fortunately, a wonderful space became available in the new Village at Wexford. It was perfect, but John and I were hesitant to put the cash needed into the new shop. But Ora stepped in and said, "But we have to do it. We have no choice. With no lease, you could lose everything you've worked for all these years. What if I put up all the money I've saved to buy a villa into the new shop?" We could not believe it. She saved us.

The new shop, Nell's at Wexford, opened in 1987 and thrived immediately with Ora in charge, making a profit in the first two years of business. Our fine staff loved working at both shops. Wexford appealed to Islanders and was a more sophisticated shop. The staff would say, "You've got to wear your *pearls* if you're working at Wexford."

Wonderful things happened to us during those two years, as both shops were nominated in 1989 for the Best Small Business of the Year. At the awards ceremony when the chairman began to read the description of the winning business, our tears of joy started to flow. We couldn't believe it! This was the pinnacle of our success because we were judged the best by our peers.

We were so happy, too, not just for ourselves but for all the wonderful people, young and old, who had ever worked at Nell's. We had always tried to hire only people whom we instinctively liked and trusted, who had essentially the same values of the importance of God, family, and serving and contributing to the community. Together we treated our customers as guests in our home, greeting them with a smile and a feeling of importance whether they bought anything or not. Our employees and customers became some of our most treasured friends, even to this day.

The next seven years zoomed by. We did not renew our new lease at Wexford because it was too high. We moved back to Harbour Town, which proved to be the perfect time to do it.

Fortunately, we were able to negotiate a new seven-year lease, planning on putting in computers, which I had fought. Not to have computers seems so stupid now, but it was an innovative move at the time, and very expensive. Very few companies had them.

But Hilton Head was changing fast, and we worked harder than ever. We had to run to keep ahead of the competition. The shop really owned us and took over our lives. There was much less time to enjoy life and relax during the holidays.

We even had to open on Thanksgiving Day when tourists and

families were everywhere on the Island. Ora and I would prepare everything ahead and freeze everything but the turkey—all the vegetables, dressing, rice, and so forth. John and the boys would be in charge of cooking the turkey with our instructions. We put a sign on each door of the shop, early in the week, reading, "Yes, we will be open on Thanksgiving Day at 10 a.m., but we will be closing at 3 p.m. to have Thanksgiving dinner with our family! We will open early Friday morning for our annual sale!"

For a long time, John thought I was working too hard, and he thought now, with business so good (1995) and a long lease, this was a good time to sell the shop. He had always wanted to restore a historic house, and for many good reasons thought it was time to move to a quieter, smaller town, close to Hilton Head.

We talked to Ora about just giving the shop to her. She surely deserved it, but Ora didn't want to own and run the shop by herself because the two of us already couldn't keep up. She wanted to move to Atlanta.

I agonized over selling, though, and leaving the Island where we had raised our children. It was home. But quickly everything began to fall into place. Someone offered to pay us cash for our shop and our *name*. The offer was too good not to give it some serious consideration. We fell in love with a historic home at 901 Prince Street, and this beautiful town of Beaufort, and its wonderful people. So all the pieces fit, and I realize now that God had this planned all along.

Do I miss the shop? Oh, yes, as I loved so much about it. However, one tends to forget the hard work and the hard times. I miss the customers who became my friends. I miss, particularly, the warmth and camaraderie of Charlene Elder, the manager, Gloria Brown, and Diane Robinson, who are still working at Nell's and keep it going. They are so dear to Ora and me.

Vainly, I miss the adrenaline rush of owning a shop, because owning a shop is much like having the lead in a Broadway play, and I was the *star* of the *show* for twenty-five years! It does not get much better than that.

I'd like to close with a Friendship Toast to all you ladies, my dear friends, who have been so good to me since I moved to Beaufort. This is a toast that Charlene's husband used to give at the close of all our shop's parties.

Life is sweet because of the friends we have made and the things
   which in common we share.
We want to live on, not because of ourselves, but because of the
   people who care.
It's in the giving and doing for somebody else, on all life's splen-
   dors depend,
and the joys in this life, when you have summed it all up, are
   found in the making of friends.

Fun for Kids

In 1964, John and I took our children—Gettys, seven; Spencer, five; and Ora Elliott, three, to resorts that specialized in first-class children's programs. Charles wanted the kids to actively participate in activities at Callaway Gardens, Georgia; Ponte Vedra, Florida; and the Buccaneer Inn in Longboat Key, Florida. We loved the idea of having grown-up time by ourselves, and the kids were excited, too.

To sample the Day Camp for kids at Callaway Gardens, we enrolled our little ones in the swimming program, advising them to watch Ora Elliott carefully because she was such a daredevil! We watched from a distance for a few minutes, and right away she swam way under the water, going under the ropes, until she got to the deeper water where her brothers were. I alerted the staff and was assured that they wouldn't take their eyes off her again.

When we returned to pick the kids up, they couldn't find an "Ora Elliott Smith." We almost collapsed, but then they quickly said they had a "Sweet Pea Smith," which was our pet name for her! We were so relieved.

We learned from the best at those three resorts. John was then put in charge to improve the Sea Pines program and later it got renamed "Fun for Kids," which is still going strong.

Social Scene

In 1964, Charles gave John and me a gourmet dinner party at the august Oglethorpe Club. Invited were ten or twelve young Savannah couples, some of whom owned a Sea Pines lot, or whose family had already built a house on the beach.

These Savannah couples opened their arms to us and invited us to formal dances and museum functions like the Masque Ball at the Telfair. We heard that some couples were ordering expensive costumes, but we knew we couldn't afford that. John thought of carrying gold-sprayed, glittery, Palmetto fronds over our eyes as masks, pretending to be Mr. and Mrs. Sea Pines. We were so surprised and happy to win first prize.

These social gatherings enriched our lives, and these couples became some of our best friends to this day.

In Sea Pines, the social scene for couples in the late '60s was almost nonexistent. If there was a party, we were all invited! We were often the youngest. The first Island party I remember was a Halloween party given on the beach by the Hands, the Seimers, and the Murtaghs, I believe. John and I went as "Two Hippies on a Honda." We almost killed ourselves in the process, riding on the dark beach on that borrowed Honda.

It Was Heaven

People often ask, what was it like raising children on Hilton Head with no doctor, no bank, and hardly any infrastructure? All I can say: "It was heaven!" The children had so much freedom to roam, explore, go fishing, go crabbing, build forts on little islands in the lagoons, not worry about traffic, go everywhere with one's dog following them, as there were no leash laws for years … the list goes on and on. They missed out on some things in the early years with no Little League, no proms, no football or basketball teams, but the gains they received for the love of beauty and reverence for nature far outweighed those things missed. All the Islanders, including the retirees, kind of looked out for each other and their children and often knew the names of their animals, too. They were so free to walk or to ride bikes everywhere.

Our German shepherd, called King, was known by everyone as the guardian of the neighborhood. He walked with Gettys, eight, and Spencer, six, to the bus stop to go to Bluffton to school. When he returned, I would ask if the boys were okay. He'd give me a dog's affirmative answer and immediately would get back in the hole he had dug in our front yard to keep an eye on the neighborhood. Most often he knew when it was time to go meet the bus in the afternoon when the children returned. He seemed to have a clock in his head. I would sometimes have to say, "King, it's time to go to pick up the kids," but not often.

And if the children were playing on the small island in the lagoon, their hideout, I would blow the car horn twice and then say, "King, please go get the kids to come on home for lunch or supper." It was a magical time.

Most of all, King was a protector of the family. One day I was sitting on the beach watching the children play in the ocean. All three of them could swim, but I didn't allow them to go out over their heads, unless John was there, too. I yelled to Spencer that he was out too far and stood up ready to rescue him. When he didn't respond, King immediately shot into the water, swam around Spencer, and pushed him with his paws onto his back toward the beach! I was amazed. Spencer was furious, but he got the message.

One night, King came to the rescue of John, too. We were awakened by King barking furiously, so John got up to see what was wrong. When John didn't come in right away, and King continued to bark, I got up and opened our kitchen door. There was John, white as a sheet, holding a Claussen's bread wrapper in his hands with King standing closely by. John breathlessly said, "I wouldn't believe it unless I had seen it myself, but a gator, up on his haunches like a dinosaur, was into our trash can with this wrapper in his mouth! King protected me from him, until he left." Needless to say, we had to have that fifteen-foot alligator moved out of our lagoon in the morning.

Gettys Learns to Fish

1965

Gettys turned into a fisherman with his new friend Andy Labrot of Savannah, who lived with his family on Beach Lagoon the entire summer. Gettys caught so many bream in the brackish waters that John taught Gettys how to clean them. He was only eight years old at the time! They were delicious, especially with grits.

In a couple of years, we gave him a handwoven shrimp net for Christmas. I wish we still had it. He learned to cast and became an entrepreneur by selling shrimp to all the neighbors for a dollar a pound, weighing them out on my kitchen scales and dripping water everywhere. No one could refuse a small, young boy with those big brown eyes!

Spencer Goes to School

Spencer was so excited to be able to go to school *at last* to begin first grade in Bluffton. In addition, he would be riding the school bus with Gettys, his big eight-year-old brother.

I could hardly wait to hear what Spencer would say about school. Instantly when he returned I was worried, when I saw his serious face. I asked right away, "How did you like school, Spencer?"

Spencer said sadly, "Well, my teacher tried as hard as she could, but she couldn't teach us to *read* today." He was crushed—so disappointed.

Integration

1965–1966

Something important happened in the schools that year—integration began. We heard that a little black girl, Pamela Cohen, was going to be in Gettys's third-grade class. Her older sister was going to be in the fifth grade at the Bluffton School, too.

Growing up as Southerners, we were *certainly* not members of the Ku Klux Klan, racists, or anything like that. Most of us mothers had been brought up playing with the nearby blacks in neighborhoods. We had been brought up to be kind and to never say "nigger," but we did use what we felt was a kinder descriptive word: "colored."

We told Gettys to be very nice to Pamela, to talk to her, and to never hurt her feelings in any way. This message was repeated by their wonderful teacher, Mrs. Peeples, as she undoubtedly instructed the children to be respectful and kind to Pamela. Often during the year, I asked Gettys how she was getting along. I asked, "Was she playing games with them at recess?"

Gettys always answered, "No, ma'am, she just runs and hugs her sister at recess." I felt so sad for those children.

At the end of the school year, I asked about who received the third-grade superlatives and was so surprised when Gettys said, "Pamela Cohen got the Best Sportsmanship Award."

I quickly asked, "But Gettys, how did she deserve that award? You told me she never participated in any of the sports."

Gettys said, "Oh, Mom, we all voted for her just because she was *black!*"

Thankfully, the mothers and teachers had done a good job instructing the white children to be kind.

The First Grave in Six Oaks

A tragic loss of a child, a first-grader, Leslie Gebhardt, the daughter of Carl and Nancy Gebhardt, saddened everyone who was here in January 1966. Leslie was a smart, sparkly, blue-eyed blonde loved by all ages and had been a beautiful angel in the Christmas play in Bluffton. Our Spencer called her his sweetheart and cried so hard to go to the funeral service, saying, "But she was my friend, Mama, not yours."

"Six Oaks" quickly was made ready for its first burial and graveside services. All the children and their parents and many retirees mourned and reached out in support of the Gebhardts and her grandparents, Mr. and Mrs. McBride, who were in charge of the Adventure Inn.

Little Leslie had pneumonia and died in her mother's arms on the way to the Beaufort Hospital. Hilton Head didn't have a hospital then. So sad.

In High Cotton

The building of the Sea Pines Plantation Golf House, designed by Corkern and Wiggins in 1966, was really an extension of the original Plantation Club. It, too, was built of traditional materials: old Savannah gray brick and bleached cypress with wide-spreading cedar shakes roofs. It was so beautiful. The Golf House also included two lounges, a snack bar, steam rooms, locker facilities, and recreation rooms.

High-coffered ceilings covered the areas housing the Pro Shop, the dining room, and the swimming pool. The pool was so modern and new because it was the indoor and outdoor type, heated for year-round use. Our children and grown-ups were so excited to experience this. We could swim from the inside pool and end up in the larger pool, outside under sunny skies. Then when hungry, we could order hamburgers, hot dogs, and more from the snack bar and eat in our bathing suits!

When the company decided to close the snack bar and open the Lake House restaurant on the other side of this complex, it came with mixed feelings. It was nice to be able to order food while you were in your bathing suits. The Lake House provided similar food with an expanded menu from the snack bar. The downside was that clothing and shoes were required.

One Saturday, Ora met Elizabeth Ramsey at the pool to swim, sunbathe, and have lunch at the Lake House. When they decided to have lunch, Elizabeth realized she had not worn any shoes. This meant she could not go into the Lake House and be served. As they approached the Lake House, Ora loaned Elizabeth a shoe so they would, hopefully, be allowed to come inside. The ladies behind the counter, with their kind and gentle faces, began to laugh out loud. No one could have turned away two seemingly clever children who were trying to obey the rules.

We all grew to love the Lake House for their food, ambience, and wonderful staff. If your father worked for the company, the food was half price, but you had to spend a whole dollar. Sometimes that was hard to do. Their French fries were to die for, and they were served in a plastic soup bowl.

The pool was a meeting and gathering place for everyone, but especially for the kids. When there were no lifeguards or parents around, someone would pull up one of the chairs to the outdoor shower. The kids would use the shower fixtures as a ladder to climb onto the roof. Then they would walk around to the roof of the indoor pool and jump into the outdoor pool. What fun!

When enough kids had arrived at the pool, there was nothing better than playing Marco Polo in the indoor pool area. Each time "Marco" was yelled out and the response of "Polo" was yelled, the echo effect in the indoor pool area made the game that much more fun and difficult.

We Islanders and guests were definitely in high cotton!

The Big Snow

The Big Snow fell for the first time in twenty years on February 8, 1968. In the wee hours that morning, the headmistress of the Academy called John. When it was still dark, Mrs. Goddard asked, "Should we have school today?"

John sleepily answered, "Why not?"

She said, "Go look outside!" He did and was surprised to see a blanket of snow on the ground.

John answered, "Call it off. The children may not ever see it here again!"

We then woke up the children, put socks on their hands for gloves, and anything we could find for their heads. I can still hear the Keds bumping around in the dryer every time they got real wet. But the children had a ball building a snowman and sliding on any incline on cookie pans. One child even had a sleigh. I even made snow ice cream—snow, vanilla, and cream!

John rushed off early, as he knew he had to be in charge of Christmas decorations for the Inn guests. In one of the brochures, his ad had promised a free visit of six days and five free nights if snow ever fell on our golf courses. So John's promise had to be kept. Many Islanders came to help him decorate a tree to brighten the tourists' spirits. An elegant breakfast was served, complete with Christmas music, and the snow had melted by mid-afternoon on the golf course. It was a *happy* time for everyone on the Island!

The First Library in a Trailer

I realize that I've neglected to tell you about the beginning of our first library in a trailer. Yes, in a trailer on Highway 278, where Carrabba's Restaurant is now. I remember being asked to serve on a library committee by Mr. Wallace Linton, the chairman. I felt so honored to serve with Mrs. J. G. (Beanie) Newhall, founder of the Audubon Park Preserve, Mr. Robert Killingsworth, Mr. I. W. Wilborn, and Mrs. Charles Rousek.

We met many times in 1968 and decided that the only way we could ever possibly afford a library was to start small and rent a trailer. So off we rode to Beaufort to look at trailers. We rented one with no furniture, but with two rooms and a bathroom. We got approved (I still can't believe we were), and we began the library at a cost of only fourteen thousand dollars plus equipment. It opened in mid-February 1969.

Since I was the only committee member with young children, the Smiths were fortunate enough to get the first library cards: numbers one, two, and three. It was so exciting for all the Island children and adults, too.

The School Bus Escapades

Sometimes, especially at night, boredom would set in among the executives, and someone would say, "I think this would be a good night to get out and steal the school bus." One memorable night, Val Hawkins was the instigator and the driver of the bus, even with a broken arm! I think it was someone's birthday. The school bus was always parked at the Maintenance Shed, which was behind the Sea Pines Center. Executives could fill up their cars with gas at the pumps, and the company cars could be serviced there. Ours was a dark green Dodge station wagon.

The school bus would go all over Sea Pines, or wherever, and would wake up its chosen passengers in the wee hours, laughing loudly and shouting, "Come on with us, we're having a party. Bring a drink and come aboard!"

One night, the busload came by our house, celebrating and noisily ringing our doorbell. John ran to the door and in a few minutes jumped on the bus. Ora Elliott's room was on the front of the house, and she got up right away and ran by our bedroom door. I sleepily said, "Who was it, Sweetie?"

She said, "Well, at first, I thought it was a bunch of drunks until I saw Mrs. Chaffin!" (She was Ora Elliott's third-grade teacher.) Oh, how we still tease Betsy and Jim Chaffin about that!

Saving the Liberty Oak

In 1971 the Liberty Oak, sitting majestically on the waters' edge of Harbour Town, was spared by John Gettys Smith's efforts and pleading to Charles to save that hundred-year-old live oak. It was going to cost Sea Pines an additional fifty thousand dollars to go around the tree and its roots during construction, so originally it was called "Smith's Folly"! Everyone teased John because the trauma around the tree's roots made many of the leaves fall off or yellow, and some fellow employees said, "Well, John, if that tree dies, there goes your job."

Thankfully, the tree survived and, oh, what a beautiful addition to the Harbour it is. We are so thankful that Hurricane Matthew didn't harm our Liberty Oak.

Children's Passion for Sports

B ack to my children growing up ...
Gettys, as I already told you, loved fishing, crabbing, and shrimping in our brackish lagoons, but then the sailing bug bit him. He wanted to take sailing lessons at South Beach, and of course, Spencer (ever the competitor) begged to take lessons, too. After arriving back home from taking both boys to their very first lesson, I got a call from the Medical Center. Gettys excitedly said, "Don't worry, Mom. Spencer has to have stitches because he was thrown off the boat and got all cut up on the oyster shells, but *the sharks didn't get him!*" I was grateful for that. I had always warned the children to get out of the water immediately if they got cut on a shell, or anything, because of the sharks.

This incident cooled Spencer's enthusiasm somewhat for this sport, but Gettys became a great sailor. The McGinty family, who lived on the beach of Beach Lagoon Road, and our family shared ownership of first a sailfish, then a sunfish, and at last a Hobie Cat. They hid the boats behind the sea oats after using them. I don't ever remember any fussing between the young people because they worked it out themselves. Sometimes, even our dog King was invited along for a boat ride.

Instead of boating, Spencer at an early age fell in love with golf. He would walk to the Golf Pro Shop, which wasn't very far, and practice putting with a few friends and adults. The adults were so good to the children and assured John and me that they weren't a bother to them. (I hope not.) As the Island grew, and we had the Heritage Tournaments, and more golf courses on the Island, these boys had a wonderful golf coach. He was a retired general, General John "Jack" Dobson. He formed the Sea Pines Academy Golf Team. They were state champions in the independent school competitions for several years. The boys learned so much from General Dobson not only about golf but good sportsmanship and manners. He encouraged the boys to go to a golf camp in the summer, and many went to Pine Needles in Southern Pines, North Carolina. Their coach there was Peggy Kirk Bell. The general gave his time voluntarily, and what a gift it was to them.

Spencer also loved all team sports, especially basketball in high school. He was a good shooter, but he was not very tall. He would often tell us, "Coach Ladd [Edwin Ladd] says I'll be *starting* tonight, but be on *time* because I won't last long."

And last, but certainly not least, Ora, loved tennis and she and Story Jones were the beginning of the legend of Bert's Girls. Dr. Bert Hodgman (a retired doctor) arrived on the Island in the early '70s and wanted to start a tennis program for girls. He had fabulous tennis credentials and had not only coached his talented tennis daughter, but led five Kalamazoo girls' teams on to championships in Michigan.

By 1973, there were nine girls on Dr. Hodgman's team. He required them to be very committed and to practice every afternoon on the Sea Pines courts after school. The children were from nine to twelve years old.

Mr. Jim Crowell offered to help Dr. Hodgman coach the girls. His drill would include serving balls to the corners, difficult to return, and reward them with ice cream if they were successful.

In high school, Ora wanted to go out for basketball, too, but Dr. Hodgman urged her not to do so. He was planning to take the girls to tournaments all over the state, even to Florida.

Dr. Hodgman and Jim Crowell took eight or nine girls in a van and would sometimes spend the night. These men demanded the girls to have good behavior, and so far I haven't learned that they misbehaved. One night, Ora said, Mr. Crowell took the older girls to see the movie *Animal House*, and he laughed so hard, right along with them. Dr. Hodgman took the youngest girl on the team, Jennifer Ahrendt, to a different movie because she wasn't old enough.

This team won at least six state championships, over schools with a huge enrollment in their high school. At that time, Sea Pines only had two hundred students from grades one through twelve.

So amazing that these retirees were willing to devote the time and expertise to bring our children up to this level.

Hofbrauhaus

In March 1973 the Hofbrauhaus restaurant opened, thanks to a $130,000 investment through the Peoples Bank of Beaufort. The average food check that month was $5.50. Imagine that!

It was popular from the very beginning of its existence. The owners were Peter Kenneweg and Robert Dickson, who had been a singing chef at the Plantation Club and years later at Roberts in Charleston. The restaurant was charming, had the German feeling, and the best Weiner Schnitzel ever, also brand new to the Lowcountry. The busboys wore Lederhosen, and our sixteen-year-old son, Gettys, worked there even though he hated to wear the outfit. He thought his legs were too skinny, and they were!

It was a great experience for him, and one night when he was very late getting home from work, he exclaimed, "Well, I know now why the Germans almost won the war!" One of the dishwashers had quit that night, and Gettys was pressed into service in the kitchen scraping plates, waiting on tables, bussing, you name it. But the new rules posted on the blackboard in the kitchen said it all:

"Yes, we will be open on the 4th of July, and there will be no more Saturday nights off for anyone for the rest of the season!"

The crew of Cruise for Conservation against the BASF plant on the Colleton River.

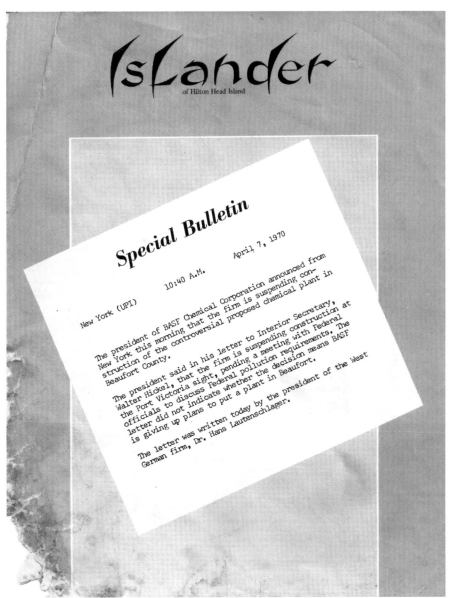

Islander
of Hilton Head Island

Special Bulletin

April 7, 1970

10:40 A.M.

New York (UPI)

The president of BASF Chemical Corporation announced from New York this morning that the firm is suspending construction of the controversial proposed chemical plant in Beaufort County.

The president said in his letter to Interior Secretary, Walter Hickel, that the firm is suspending construction at the Port Victoria sight, pending a meeting with Federal officials to discuss Federal pollution requirements. The letter did not indicate whether the decision means BASF is giving up plans to put a plant in Beaufort.

The letter was written today by the president of the West German firm, Dr. Hans Lautenschlager.

Special bulletin on the cover of the Islander magazine about defeating the BASF plant.

John Gettys Smith, Nelle Smith, Ora Smith with a couple of protest signs with Peter Ovens sitting down.

Walter J. Hickel shaking hands with Captain Dave on the shrimp boat.

Gettys Smith with his dog, King, shrimping.

*John Newcombe and Rod Laver at
the Tournament of Champions.*

John Newcombe returning a shot at the CBS Tennis Classic.

First Annual

CBS TENNIS CLASSIC

March 21 - 24th, 1972

SEA PINES RACQUET CLUB
Sea Pines Plantation
Hilton Head Island, South Carolina

SEA PINES PLANTATION COMPANY in cooperation with WORLD CHAMPIONSHIP TENNIS will sponsor the CBS TENNIS CLASSIC on Tuesday, Wednesday, Thursday and Friday, March 21, 22, 23, 24, 1972. The sixteen top WORLD CHAMPIONSHIP Tennis professionals will compete for Forty-Seven Thousand Five Hundred Dollars ($47,500) in prize money. The site will be the Sea Pines Racquet Club in the nationally-acclaimed resort community of SEA PINES PLANTATION, Hilton Head Island, South Carolina.

Ticket Application

TICKET SALES WILL BE LIMITED

PATRON TICKET — Reserved preferred seating in patron section and admission to Racquet Club during Tournament. Includes invitation to a party for the players. Limited number available.

_____ Patron @ $35.00 each $_____

GENERAL ADMISSION SEASON TICKET — Individual tickets for admission to entire event. No reserved seats. Tickets are transferable.

_____ Season Tickets @ $25.00 per Set $_____

GENERAL ADMISSION DAILY TICKETS —

Tuesday _____	_____	@ $ 7.00 each $_____
Wednesday _____	_____	@ $ 7.00 each $_____
Thursday _____	_____	@ $ 7.00 each $_____
Friday _____	_____	@ $10.00 each $_____

Enclosed is my check or money order for: TOTAL $_____

ALL CHECKS PAYABLE TO "CBS TENNIS CLASSIC"

NAME_____

ADDRESS_____

CITY_____   STATE_____   ZIP CODE_____

Mail this application and check to: CBS TENNIS CLASSIC
SEA PINES TOURNAMENT OFFICE
HARBOUR TOWN CLUB HOUSE
HILTON HEAD ISLAND, SOUTH CAROLINA 29928
(803) 785-3395

(Tickets will be mailed immediately upon receipt of application and check)

NOTE: For reservations for accommodations, write or call the SEA PINES RESERVATIONS OFFICE, Hilton Head Inn, Hilton Head Island, South Carolina 29928. (803) 785-3322. Please indicate that you plan to attend the CBS TENNIS CLASSIC.

First Annual CBS Tennis Classic flyer.

John Gettys Smith, chairman of the first Heritage Golf Classic, shaking Arnold Palmer's hand with the unfinished Harbour Town lighthouse in the background, 1969.

Family Circle Cup party event. L TO R: *John Gettys Smith, Jack Jones, John Curry and John Moreno.*

*Early aerial photograph of the 17th and 18th holes at The Heritage Classic.
The crowds were limited to 5000 spectators in the first tournaments.*

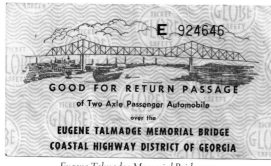

E 924646

GOOD FOR RETURN PASSAGE
of Two Axle Passenger Automobile
over the
EUGENE TALMADGE MEMORIAL BRIDGE
COASTAL HIGHWAY DISTRICT OF GEORGIA

Eugene Talmadge Memorial Bridge pass.

1969
HERITAGE
SEA PINES
PLANTATION
Void If Detached

1969 Heritage food ticket.

HISTORICAL TOUR OF HILTON HEAD ISLAND

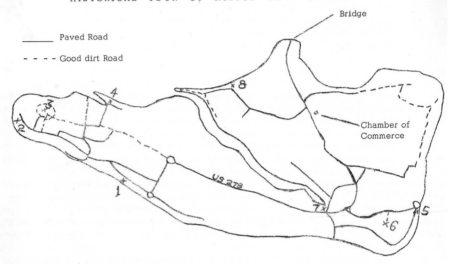

1. Go the the William Hilton Inn first, where there are exhibits on the over-all history of the Island.

2. Braddock's Point: Civil War Battery (exhibit panel on high sand dune, ocean side)

3. Baynard Ruins: Ante-bellum Plantation House.

4. Calibogue Sound: Water-way of coastal war and trade.

5. Fort Walker, Battle of Port Royal, Camp Welles, and Experimental cannon.

6. Fort Sherman: Union Army Earthworks.

7. Zion Chapel of Ease: Ante-bellum Graveyard.

8. Spanish Wells: Fresh water source possibly used during the Spanish occupation of this area in the 16th century.

This map was prepared by the CAROLINA LOWCOUNTRY HISTORICAL AND CULTURAL FOUNDATION, a chartered, non-profit corporation established by the resort owners of this Island to research, preserve, and exhibit the history of this region.

Historical tour of Hilton Head Island.

Lauretta Holmes wedding. L TO R: *Michele Merritt, Diane Fecher, Nelle Smith, Spencer Smith, Lauretta Holmes, John Gettys Smith, Ora Smith and Annie Lou Holmes.*

Nelle Smith and Ora Smith in front of Nell's Harbour Shop.

Dr. Spencer McCants with his Cabbage Patch boys.

Indoor/outdoor swimming pool at the Plantation Club.

Bronze alligator at the Plantation Club.

John Gettys and Nelle Smith at the grand opening of the Sea Pines Plantation Club.

A family enjoys the local sport of crabbing at Hilton Head Island, South Carolina. The catch goes into many of the famous Low Country recipes that are part of the traditional menus at the William Hilton Inn, a year 'round resort facility. (The Smith family)

A gull's-eye view of poolside loungers at the William Hilton Inn, Hilton Head Island, South Carolina. The Inn is an 80 room year 'round facility. Carolina low country dishes and seafood caught in local bays and creeks, are features on the Inn's menus. 1969

Saturday night oyster roast-buffet at the ocean front William Hilton Inn, Hilton Head Island, South Carolina, a 134 unit year 'round inn, featuring Carolina Low Country dishes and seafood caught in local bays and creeks on its menus.

Palmetto Bay Marina—A complete marina located on deepwater Broad Creek, just southeast of 4 second flasher "32" where the Intracoastal Waterway meets Calibogue Sound. Owned by the Sea Pines Plantation Company, developers of the Island's nationally acclaimed resort community, Sea Pines Plantation and the William Hilton Inn.

The William Hilton Inn, Hilton Head Island, SC. Looking in from the Atlantic Ocean at the new 80-unit William Hilton Inn. In addition to superb cuisine, the inn features two pools, putting green, badminton, tennis, golf, dancing, oyster roasts, free island tours. Master Innkeeper Wesley W. Graves is your Host.

The Front Beach. An ocean-front forest of stately sea pines on historic Hilton Head Island. The island's 30,000 acres of natural beauty include 13 miles of unbroken white sand beaches, abundant wildlife, and a year 'round subtropical climate. This view within Sea Pines Plantation.

The 4½ miles of uncrowded beach is protected by sand dunes covered with sea oats: the sand is firm enough for bicycling

The first annual fashion show fundraiser for Sea Pines Academy.

Sea Pines Academy girl's tennis team. L TO R *(front row): Carmen Hawkins, Jana Walker, Ora Smith and Jan Geiger.* L TO R *(back row): Kim Isaacs, Robin Scherer, Dr. Bert Hodgman, June Ahrendt and Kathy Love.*

Sea Pines Academy golf team. L TO R *(excluding the adults): Earle Palmer, David O'Quinn, David Rourke, Spencer Smith, Drew Butler, Tom (Tab) Bailey and Tom Cornelia.*

The Island Packet, Tuesday, May 15, 1979

Dr. Bert Hodgman stands with his Sea Pines Academy state championship tennis team before the group tore asunder all comers in the independent school state tournament on Hilton Head. This group has won 127 consecutive individual matches in regular-season play, and for two consecutive years have been state champions, placing all nine teams in the tournament finals. Standing from left are June Ahrendt, Robin Scherer and Katharine Love. Seated, from left, are Carmen Hawkins, Kim Isaacs, Ora Elliott Smith and Sue Hilton. (Photo by Barbara Hefty).

Champions

Sea Pines Academy girl's tennis team.

Andy Labrot and Gettys Smith showing off their catch at the Lake House lagoon.

Charles Fraser's reunion birthday party at the Sea Pines Plantation Club.

Sea Pines executives in the first Heritage Classic jackets.
L TO R: *Wally Palmer, Bill Dyer, John Gettys Smith, Don O'Quinn and Franz Meier.*

Bust of Charles E. Fraser with the Harbour Town lighthouse in the background.

Plaque for Charles E. Fraser.

Bust of Charles E. Fraser.

Walkway to the beach in Sea Pines. This was one of Hideo Sasaki's suggestions to Charles Fraser in the land planning stage for the company.

SEA PINES COMPANY

HILTON HEAD ISLAND, S. C.

telephone - area code 803 - 785 - 3333

September 8, 1971

On every hand good good words of praise continue to come in on the dash, style, and efficiency of the Tennis Tournament. Your good sense of quality once more was visibly displayed to the World.

HB
Please Congratulations on a superb new look on the Southeast Sports scene.

Mr. John G. Smith
Vice President-Public Relations
Sea Pines Company
Hilton Head Island, S. C. 29928

Dear John:

You have received a copy of a letter to me from Howard Reifsnyder of CBS Sports which was most flattering of the hospitality and cooperation given CBS by Sea Pines and which specifically mentioned the contributions made by you, Donald O'Quinn, Pete Collins and Nancy Smith.

We all know that once again we at Sea Pines have innovated and scored a success. I want you to know that I am most grateful and appreciative of the persistent hard work that went into making the CBS Tournament of Tennis Champions a major, nationally-acclaimed sports event. Your imagination and leadership were certainly the catalysts without which the undertaking would have been impossible.

With cordial good wishes,

Sincerely yours,

Charles E. Fraser
President

/db

The Sea Pines Company, through its affiliates, The Sea Pines Plantation Company and The Lighthouse Beach Company, owns and operates a 5,000 acre ocean front resort community located on Hilton Head Island, South Carolina. Facilities include three championship 18 hole golf courses, a tennis club, the ocean front Hilton Head Inn, the Plantation Club, famous for its southern cuisine and the well appointed Palmetto Bay Marina.

Charles Fraser's letter to John Gettys Smith.

1968 snow on Hilton Head in the Smith's backyard. L TO R *Gettys Smith, Charlie Fraser, Ora Smith, Margaret McGinty, Spencer Smith, Leigh McGinty and Rupert McGinty.*

1968 snow on Hilton Head in the Smith's side yard. L TO R *(standing) Rupert McGinty, Charlie Fraser, Thornton Withers, Ora Smith and Margaret McGinty.* L TO R *(sitting) Leigh McGinty, Adams Withers, Gettys Smith and Spencer Smith.*

*John Gettys Smith at a Halloween party,
dressed up as Luke Taylor.*

4th of July beach party. L TO R *Nelle and John
Smith with Judy and Dan Bradley.*

4th of July beach party. L TO R *Jenny Lynn Bradley
with Larry and Dede Austin.*

4th of July beach party. L TO R *Merrill Barringer, Kay McDonnell,
Paul Barringer, Ed McDonnell and Helen Cork.*

First nativity at St. Luke's Episcopal Church

*Spencer Smith leading the first junior choir
at St. Luke's Episcopal Church.*

*Nelle Smith dressed up in a nurse's uniform for an
adoption party for the Cabbage Patch babies.*

*Penny Hall in the Sea Pines Academy
fashion show fundraiser.*

Jean Bates at the Sea Pines Academy Fashion Show.

Ocean Gate at Sea Pines.

The foot bridge on Beach Lagoon Road.

Stan and Margie Smith

It seems to me that we were always close friends with Stan and Margie. After all, they announced their engagement on our sofa, one happy night a long time ago. (It will always be named "The Stan Smiths' sofa"!)

John and I noticed right away the excitement and joy in their eyes. John asked then, "What's going on with you two tonight?"

Stan, with his arm around Margie, said, "Well, I just asked Margie to marry me and she said, 'Yes!'"

We all screamed and hugged each other. Afterward, we went to the Plantation Club for dinner to celebrate.

From that time on, we've celebrated the births and weddings of their children and ours. What a privilege that has been. I know we must share some Smith ancestors because we are so close. They have supported us in both sad and joyous times. They are true friends.

The Swing Bridge

1974

The Hilton Head Island swing bridge was struck by a barge, which stopped all traffic across the bridge. After the news spread, all the natives and tourists were stranded on the Island, and rumors of what happened were flying. The funniest one was that the captain of the barge asked the bridge keeper if the barge could continue its voyage. The reply was, "Hell, no, man, you're in a heap of trouble!"

It took the Army Corps of Engineers two weeks to build a pontoon bridge (I, too, wondered how we ever won a war!). One of my full-time employees lived in Bluffton and was stuck on the other side. The shopkeepers hoped that the tourists stuck on the Island didn't run out of money.

One or two pregnant ladies were taken by helicopter to Savannah to deliver their babies because there was no hospital on the Island at that time.

The Pioneers

I still marvel at the courage of the couples who had the nerve or the pioneering spirit to start a business of their own here in the early 1960s. After all, there were only twelve year-round families living in Sea Pines in 1963, no Palmetto Dunes, no Hilton Head Plantation, no Port Royal Plantation, no Long Cove, and virtually no infrastructure. Certainly, the McGintys, who moved here in 1951, were the earliest pioneers. Pete came as an architect, and Aileen taught all grades in the one-room schoolhouse at Honey Horn.

Oh, the families like the Capins, who opened the first pharmacy; the Perrys, who opened the first printing company; the George Moores, who opened the Bamboo Cage, a store for office supplies; and the architects and the construction companies of Robert Woods, C. J. Jones, Robert Graves, Farris Highsmith. There are so many firsts—Espy Concrete Company; the first insurance companies, Carswell Insurance and Palmer and Cay Insurance; and Hilton Head Interiors, the first interior decorating business, owned by Helen and Bill Cork was located where the Santa Fe Restaurant is now. I wish I could remember and write about all those early businesses.

In the formative years of the '60s, most of these businesses were definitely depending on Sea Pines' success, because mainly we were the only show in town.

Fin 'N Feather

Our first fast-food business was the Fin 'N Feather, which naturally served fried shrimp, fried chicken, and French fries in Coligny Plaza, near where the Frosty Frog and Pizza is now, and very near the Island Theater. The Kuechlers bought this business in the early '70s and all the kids remember their smart ninth-grade son who took eleventh- and twelfth-grade classes.

When our son Spencer worked there, I was flabbergasted to learn that he solely cooked all the food when ordered, took in all the money for what was served, and even cleaned up everything before closing. He had never cooked at home, and had certainly never cleaned up the kitchen. All the boys wanted to work there, too, and they learned responsibility from their experience. It was a take-out store, and the food was actually good, we thought. Coligny Plaza was well on the way toward being our downtown.

The First Movie Theater

In 1972 the Paul Ramsey family opened the Island Theater. Paul told me that he contacted Norris Richardson and said he wanted to open a business on Hilton Head. Paul thought a shop selling underwear, socks, and so forth would save Islanders from having to drive to Savannah or Beaufort. But Mr. Richardson said, "No, don't do that. Open a movie theater instead." So Paul did, as he wanted to move his family to the Island. His wife, Gretchen, an artist, taught art at Sea Pines Academy, and their son, Craig, and daughter, Elizabeth, became good friends of all our children.

Craig said that Bill Cornelia, a noted photographer, took a picture of Craig and Tom Cornelia throwing popcorn in their mouths on opening day. I remember that happy picture. So many friends worked there: our Spencer and Drew Butler loved their jobs of selling movie tickets, making and eating the popcorn, and more, plus seeing all the movies. They probably ate up all of the profits!

The John Gardner Tennis Camp

Carmel Valley, California

In the early 1970s, tennis camps were beginning to boom, and John convinced Charles that Sea Pines should definitely have an excellent tennis camp. John researched the best ones and Charles recommended that our tennis pro, John Baker, and his wife, Carolyn, John, and I go to the John Gardner Tennis Camp in Carmel Valley, California.

We were so excited to be going to this luxurious place that attracted the rich and famous internationally. It was rated as the best, five-star, and we took our best tennis outfits and each of our warm-up suits.

Each couple had a small, cozy, elegant cottage. Early in the morning, there was a knock on our door, a fire was lit in the fireplace, and a delicious full breakfast was served on a silver tray, silver cream and sugar, and lovely china. So elegant!

The first evening we arrived, the staff had a lovely cocktail and dinner party for all the guests. After that very party, the staff advised us which tennis group we would be in the next morning. I think there were four to six groups. Group I was ranked as excellent. John and John Baker were to report there, but John didn't last in that group—it really was for the pros! After all, John Baker, who grew up in England, had many tennis trophies. Carolyn was assigned to

Group II which was good, and John was reassigned to Group II as well. I was a novice and assigned to the bottom group from the beginning. There was not a huge crowd of players, perhaps twenty-four or thirty people. They were all very friendly, nice, and *rich*.

On the second day of classes, all the ladies had on different warm-up outfits. We invented the white lie that we had packed our warm-up suits in one large suitcase, which had never arrived. Luckily, the guests' clothes were washed and pressed each day, if needed.

After rigorous lessons in the morning, we were served a fabulous lunch, a different soufflé dessert every day. Then naptime and classes again in the afternoon. Afterward, we could soak in hot tubs, brand new and located all around the cottages. We would then shower and dress for cocktails and dinner. What a life.

There was much talk about who would be in the tournament at the end of the week. I didn't worry about it because I assumed that the two best men and the two best ladies would play against each other. That was not the case. John Baker was the best male player, and I assumed I was chosen as the worst female, or next to worse, and was paired with him. The other couple was the second best male player and a lady from Scotland, who was better than I, as his partner!

I was frightened to death about it as every one of the guests and staff would be watching. John Baker kept reassuring me not to worry, that he'd try to get all the shots except those that were served to me. He kept saying to me, "All you have to do is hold your racquet back and try to return the serve." (I had my hair done to look as good as possible before we played.)

Well, believe it or not, John and I won the tournament. The video taken of us is hilarious. I seem to be constantly "checking my grip" and John is moving "like crazy" everywhere to back me up.

Most of the guests wanted to come back to camp the following year at the same time, so that we could keep up with each other. We were flattered that they wanted us, but we knew Sea Pines wouldn't treat us to the John Gardner Tennis Camp a second time. We didn't dare divulge that fact!

Sea Pines University Tours

It is more unbelievable to me now that a total of 160 employees, wives, husbands, singles, and so on spent an entire week flying on two chartered Ozark Airlines DC-9-30 planes all over the United States, visiting the best resorts with lectures and guides all along the way, with fabulous food and lodging on an all-expenses-paid trip! Imagine that—then or now!

Charles had envisioned these tours for a long time, despite the gigantic costs of doing so. He felt that the experiences would broaden our education, produce new creative ideas, stretch our imaginations, enrich our lives, and far outweigh the costs.

At that time, it was already planned for the Sea Pines Company to go public on the stock exchange shortly after the trip. I remember my father said, "Nelle, you and John go ahead and take advantage of this trip, because the shareholders will never allow a trip like this again." We definitely agreed.

John and I didn't fly together at that time because of our children, so I was on the "A" trip (which was subdivided into A-1 and A-2). John was placed in Group B (subdivided into B-1 and B-2).

I roomed with Susie Larsen. We left early in the morning on two chartered buses with a luggage truck traveling behind us to Savannah to board our plane. Our group experienced the northern town

125

route of flying to Denver, then were met by two buses and a new luggage truck to Vail. It was so picturesque and beautiful with snow on the mountains.

It was the first time I had ever seen that part of our country. That night we had wonderful food at restaurants all within walking distance of the hotels. It was like walking in a Christmas card or village with all the lights twinkling on the snow.

The next day, our group went to the Breckenridge town area, then were taken on a ski lift over the slopes, had lectures by developers, then back on buses with the luggage truck traveling behind. Oh, I forgot to tell you that a warning was posted each time we loaded on the buses saying, "Please load buses according to your group number, A-1 or A-2, and color. This will determine which hotel you go to and whether you will ever see your luggage again!" As far as I know, no luggage was lost.

After we returned to Denver by buses, we flew on our plane to Los Angeles with cocktails and dinner on the plane. The next day, we heard a lecture by a University of Southern California professor on the elderly needs in our society and then were taken to the most viable new communities, then to lunch at Marina del Rey. The next day, we were taken to many various quality developments near Irvine.

We then took off by plane in the late afternoon to San Francisco, treated with snacks and cocktails aboard. Then we all stayed at the Holiday Inn on Fisherman's Wharf. We had a free night to eat anywhere we wanted.

The next day, we had many more tours of developments in the area and elegant dinners at specified places. Time just flew by!

John was on the B-1 or B-2 tour, seventy-two strong on two planes and one luggage truck. John's group took a more southern route, flying to Houston, San Diego, Monterey, Carmel, then to San Francisco, where we all had the time of our lives!

Can any of us even imagine how expensive these tours were? Those of us who went on the Sea Pines University Tours will never forget this incredible experience, and the fun and enjoyment we had. In retrospect, the tours accomplished all of Charles's ideas. It was indeed another "chance of a lifetime."

John Begins His Own Public Relations Company

John Gettys Smith Associates

DECEMBER 20, 1973

I definitely did not want John to resign from Sea Pines, and neither did his mother. We pleaded and pleaded, but John was determined to do it in late 1973. He was worried about the Sea Pines Company with its debt, and he had proven himself with his success promoting the Heritage and the tennis tournaments. He felt he could do the same for other clients, and this was the right time.

Moreover, John had recently received the top national award in the field of resorts and accommodations by the Discovery America Travel Organization (DATO). At this same annual meeting in Lake Placid, New York, John was presented the Order of the CORTE (Council of Regional Travel Executives) award as the "man who has contributed more than any other to the travel industry in the South." I was in the audience at Lake Placid and had tears in my eyes. I had no idea he would receive this award, nor did John.

Charles actually encouraged John to begin his own business, John Gettys Smith Associates, by being so generous to him. He gave John, for a limited time, all of the Sea Pines accounts: Sea Pines Plantation, Hilton Head Plantation Company, Amelia Island Plantation Company, Palmas del Mar (Puerto Rico), River Hills Plantation (South

ORDER OF THE CORTE AWARD

THE SOUTH REGION

TO

JOHN GETTYS SMITH

PRESENTED BY: DOUGLAS O. BENTON

THE ORDER OF THE CORTE AWARD FOR THE SOUTH REGION GOES TO JOHN GETTYS SMITH OF SEA PINES COMPANY, SOUTH CAROLINA. A VICE PRESIDENT OF SEA PINES FOR OVER 10 YEARS, HE HAS BROUGHT THIS CORPORATION, AS WELL AS THE ENTIRE SOUTH, INTO NATIONAL ATTENTION AS A TOURISM DESTINATION AREA.

A MAN USED TO RECIEVING AWARDS AND HONORS, HE HAS DESERVED EVERY ONE OF THEM, INCLUDING THIS RECOGNITION IN THE ORDER OF THE CORTE. HIS RECENT ELECTION AS CHAIRMAN OF THE SOUTH CAROLINA TRAVEL CONFERENCE ATTESTS TO HIS MAJOR ACCOMPLISHMENTS IN THAT STATE WHICH HAVE BENEFITED HIS WHOLE REGION.

A PROFESSIONAL IN EVERY SENSE OF THE WORD, MR. SMITH HAS EFFECTIVELY PROMOTED THE SOUTH FOR MANY YEARS AND HAS SIGNIFICANTLY CONTRIBUTED TO TOURISM DEVELOPMENT WITHIN THE ENTIRE UNITED STATES.

Order of the Corte Award to John Gettys Smith.

Carolina), Big Canoe (Georgia), and Brandermill (Virginia). In addition, John kept his own office in the executive building of the Sea Pines Company.

Charles valued all that John had accomplished for the Sea Pines Company and wanted him to succeed. In addition, Charles knew that John's work ethic meant that he would take care of all of the Sea Pines accounts in the interim, and it would be a smooth transition.

John was so grateful and said, "I cannot overstate my appreciation of this offer from Charles. Needless to say, having the Sea Pines properties as my first clients is a tremendous start and is most warmly appreciated. I am very excited about establishing my own agency, continuing to work with the very fine people in the Sea Pines Company, and the prospect of working here and off the Island."

John was very successful with his own company, too, and didn't retire until 1998. His final resort client was the Sea Island Company, known mostly as the famous Cloisters. I always felt so proud that John had a fabulous career with the *newest* resort, Sea Pines, and one of the *oldest* outstanding resorts in the United States, the Sea Island Company, too.

Giving Fraser His Due

Pioneer Deserves Local Recognition
Written by John Gettys Smith;
published in the Island Packet, *July 19, 1992*

"A prophet is not without honor except"—perhaps on his own Island.

Charles E. Fraser and his community developments have been honored by the most august organizations in the real estate development industry, as well as by national and international architectural and environmental organizations.

Every governor of South Carolina since the 1950s has recently written official letters of praise for his contributions to our Island, our state and our nation. Two of these men presently serve as our U.S. senators.

On his recent birthday, he was singularly honored by the prestigious Urban Land Institute by being named an emeritus member—one of only nine so named in its 75-year history.

The lighthouse he conceived at Harbour Town is an internationally recognized symbol of not only Sea Pines, his award-winning community, but also cited by the ULI for the "Best Large-Scale Community in America" award. Harbour Town is likewise individually an award-winning landmark on our Island and famed throughout the U.S. and much of the world.

These things are points of honor for all of us.

Few Islanders who lived here in 1972 would be here without the pioneering, high-quality land planning and development which Charles Fraser originated and persisted in pursuing against all odds. Others were also instrumental in making the revolutionary concepts a reality and the success for which Sea Pines and Hilton Head Island are so well known, but it cannot be denied that Charles Fraser was the catalyst, the original dreamer whose visions brought us all here to pursue our own dreams.

Charles has not done all things perfectly. At last count, that places him in the same category with all the rest of us in the world. He is not noted for patience or, at times, politeness. He has irritated many along the way. He has other failures and shortcomings. So does everyone else. Nevertheless, no one can denigrate the excellence of the achievements which the company he founded and developed have achieved for our Island, our state and our nation. Without him, they would not be and we would not be here.

There are many companies and individuals on Hilton Head Island who have made millions of dollars as a result of all these things. Almost every company and all of the people who work for each of them, large and small, owe him a great debt. So do each of us who have come here, first as tourists, and later as proud residents of this special place we call home.

Our local prophet is so far without honor only here on our Island, despite the fact that he is considered by millions to be the modern-day founder of this place as we know it today.

No place on Hilton Head Island honors this man to whom we owe so much.

As a token of repayment for the debt we all owe, a group of Island residents—Maynard Barker, Jim Richardson, Bill Carson,

Jim Baxter, Paul Franks, Tommy Austin, Ralph Ballentine, Wayne Edwards and I—have organized an effort to erect a statue of Charles. Ralph and Wayne are volunteering their time and talent to create the statue. We need your help to make it a reality.

We have approximately $18,000 in the fund so far. We need approximately $60,000. Please send your check made payable to The Charles E. Fraser Statue Fund. Also, please write a paragraph or more about what Charles has meant to you and to Hilton Head Island. I want to compile a book of these quotes to present to Charles and his family.

Please send your check and your testimonial today. Be part of honoring our local prophet on his and our own Island.

Retrospective

Fourth of July Beach Parties
Written by John Gettys Smith,
published in the Island Scene, *Autumn 1995*

Nelle and John's Fourth of July party on the beach has long been an Island tradition. No one is quite sure when it first began, but it must be at least twenty years ago. I started our annual Fourth of July beach party way back when because I wanted to be sure we didn't have to go to a dressy brunch somewhere and spoil an otherwise perfect opportunity to spend a casual holiday on one of the prettiest beaches in the world—ours.

Brunches are fine things, but they do require getting all dressed up, which can be fun, and they tend to take one's whole day. There is no time to do anything else in the morning before getting ready to go. A three-hour slice is taken out of the middle of the day with drinking, often eating delicious food and chatting with some most attractive people, some who are real and true friends. Frequently, they are held in settings that would make Martha Stewart drool. But afterwards it is nap time and the day is gone.

I really have nothing against brunches, but the problem is when such a splendid event takes place on a day when it's great just to put on a bathing suit and casually enjoy all of those same ingredients on the beach in Sea Pines—a setting designed by the Good Lord, the

Master Decorator Himself. In defense of that opportunity, I came up with our beach party.

Our first Fourth of July parties were held where the bridge and path next to our Beach Lagoon house opens onto the beach. The section of beach paralleling Beach Lagoon Road is very special. There grow the towering pines, their crowns sculpted by the salty sea breezes, which gave Sea Pines its name. They are the tallest pines along the beach, and beneath them, for some reason, grow some of the lushest combinations of palmetto, live oak, magnolia, cassina, wax myrtle, and other natural vegetation around our island. The tree-lined beach stretches away in a crescent toward the south. The beach is wide and firm.

The tourists who pack the parking lot at the Beach Club pour out onto that beach and, perhaps because they are accustomed to crowded, noisy cities up North, settle down elbow to elbow on whatever, and noisily re-create as best they can those conditions on a Carolina sea island. Fortunately for us, they almost never spread out beyond where the parking lot path funnels them.

Our party has been held on the beach behind the Bradleys' house every year since those very first ones. The Bradleys are warm and wonderful Southern ladies and gentlemen. Whichever Bradley is in residence—they rotate the three summer months—is our co-host for the Fourth of July party.

Since the 200th anniversary of the national birthday back in '76, I have annually made a theme figure, from five to six feet high, fashioned on chicken wire, covered with newspaper and painted appropriately. The first was the Statue of Liberty. Other ladies have included Tammy Faye and Hillary. The men have ranged from Perot and Schwarzkopf to OJ. The theme is always a secret. One year, a lovely, talented young lady named Starr sprang from a cardboard cake in tights and top hat on cue and sang "The Star-Spangled Banner" and "Dixie"!

Many of our guests have attended every party since the beginning. Other newer friends have been added each year, and they combine to make the event a very special occasion. Guests are invited to bring their choice of beverages, ice, favorite picnic comestible, children of any age and their normally charming selves in a holiday, festive spirit.

Bruz and Kitty Boardman are originals and add their gourmet touch and their tent. Bruz is an excellent photographer as well. Each year they put together a handsome scrapbook of the day. That collection is spread out each year for friends, old and new, to thumb through, reminisce and enjoy.

Marguerite and Bill Bird have never missed. Bill and I have been tennis partners since well before our first Fourth of July party, and our children grew up together here. Great friends!

Ruthie and Berry Edwards have always been regulars as well as very special friends who, since last winter, live just across the street. Great neighbors as well!

Kay and Ed McDonnell fly in every year from wherever they are—New York, Connecticut, London. Ed has been president of Seagram's International for a number of years and annually hosts a fortnight of parties at Wimbledon, which he leaves to come to ours. Ed joins our tennis foursome when he is here.

Newer friends such as David and Becky Pardue and Jim and JoAnn DeVira have added their attractive ingredients in recent years since moving to the Island. Jim and I actually have been friends for a quarter century (!) since he was advertising manager for *Southern Living* in New York. Before he finally retired—at a youthful-looking age!—he was publisher of that fine magazine. The DeViras and their wonderful house are featured in the July '95 issue of *Southern Accents*.

Other friends who also made the party include Dwight and Susie Emanuelson. Dwight is a long-time tennis buddy, as is Will Bridgers, a newer Island resident and a good friend who, with his wife, Pluma, are regulars. Angus and Bev Cotton always bring the American flag (there are also Confederate ones!)

Everyone on the invitation list brings his own special quality of charm. There is no way to name them all without printing the list! But they include Susan and Richard Woods, Margaret and Walter Greer, Trisha and Bobby Freeman, Bubba and Claire McKenzie, Pete and Jeanie Hall, Helen Cork, Paul and Merrill Barringer, Barbara Kappler, Lottie Woodward, Charles and Mary Fraser, Anne and Tom Webster, Caroline and Bill Bowen, Scott and Margaret Richardson, Paul and Margaret Franks—all oldtime islanders.

More recent great additions to our community such as Dupper and Ellen Dupps are normally here, but were in Italy this year. A first this year was the "Bicycle Arrival Parade" led by Leslie and J. R. Richardson, Hester and Bobby Hodde, Betty Hodde, Melissa and Bob Faught, Fran and Rip Rose, Merrill and Randy Light, McBrier and Mike Maloney, and all their children!

Our grown children, Spencer and Ora Elliott Smith, are always regulars and lifelong friends of their elder attendees. Add old friends like Helen and Brantley Harvey from Beaufort and Bess and Tom Lawton from Allendale and newer friends such as the Reverend Greg and Meredith Kronz, with such great friends of long standing like Diane and Con Fecher, and you have a tremendous recipe for a fabulous party.

Sad News

I remember receiving the sad news on December 15, 2002, that Charles had died. Joe Fraser called John and asked this poignant question, "John, do you think there will be enough room to bury Charles under his bust at Harbour Town? The family thinks Charles would like that burial site."

John quoted the dimensions of the area and offered to call Mark King, who was in charge of that area of Sea Pines when the bust was dedicated. Thankfully, there was room for Charles.

On that cold day before the funeral service, a small group of us gathered at the burial site with the family and the Reverend Holland Clark leading us in a Committal Service for the Dead.

The funeral service was so beautiful and celebrated the life of a great man who had affected all of us in the vast crowd of mourners.

I was so worried about John, because he'd had a stroke in November, and although all of his faculties had returned, he was vulnerable and very emotional. Those former employees, all sitting together, presented an unforgettably sad moment.

Moving to Beaufort

In 1996 we sold Nell's Harbour Shop and moved to Beaufort to live and restore an antebellum home at 901 Prince Street. At first I thought I would die from homesickness, but I tried to hide it from John and others. John fit like a glove into this historic, beautiful town and the warm welcoming of old and new friends, but it took some time for me to feel at home. Almost every day, after meeting new friends early to walk around the waterfront and the Point, I would go into the original St. Peter's Historic Church to pray and cry. God answered my prayers, and I fell in love with Beaufort, too. Friends wrapped their arms around us. I'm so happy, and I am exactly where I should be at this time of my life.

John immediately became active in every aspect of life in Beaufort: the Beaufort Historic Foundation, serving as president, and began the first yearly oyster roast to secure new members; he was chairman of the Lafayette Soiree; he revived and established the Old Commons Neighborhood; he became chairman of the annual "Night on the Town" and Christmas tree lighting, as he had done on Hilton Head; and won the Volunteer of the Year award. At the same time, he continued his work of designing gardens for clients, and the two church gardens at St. Helena's and the Wesley United Methodist Church.

On August 24, 2006, John and I closed on a contract to buy a house on the river at 8 Seabrook Point. It was an exciting day with our son

Spencer as our attorney, and our daughter, Ora, as our Realtor. The market was so good at that time, and our 901 Prince Street home had been appraised at $2.5 million. We planned to put up the house for sale immediately after signing, as we were afraid someone else would buy the river property, which had a dock and a beautiful river view, before we sold our house. We didn't owe anything on our historic home, so we weren't fearful. I remember the banker who loaned us the money to buy the river house said, "Please don't sell this house in less than sixty days because we've given you such a good loan." Little did he know that the housing market would crash and it would take us eight and a half years, until December 15, 2014, to sell the property.

On September 11, 2006 we received a terrifying message from Adelaide Corkern on the phone, telling us that Spencer had suffered an aortic aneurysm and was on the way by ambulance to St. Joseph's Hospital in Savannah. She said, "Don't worry about the children. Melanie Warner and I are looking after them until Ellen's parents arrive. Come to the emergency room at St. Joseph's right away." We sang hymns and recited scripture and prayed through our tears all the way to Savannah.

Sadly, Spencer died in the operating room two days later, September 13. Losing a child is devastating, so out of order. It's a permanent wound and void in our lives. It took me years to write about this loss, and I don't think I can share many details with you readers, even now, as it's still painful. My faith was tested, but thankfully it is stronger than ever now.

I have learned to concentrate on my many happy memories. I am fortunate that Spencer was a good son, brother, friend to others, husband, father, attorney, active in giving to the community, and a faithful member of St. Luke's Church. No parent can ask for more than that, but oh, how we miss him.

Spencer and Ellen Smith with Cotter and Christine.
Samantha Smith was born two years later.

Ellen continues to be a wonderful mother to their children, and they are such a joy to Ora and Gettys and me.

In May 2007 Ellen and the children moved to Summerville. They found a nice house in the same neighborhood as her parents. Their moving away at that time was so sad to John and me, because her parents were the only people there who knew and loved Spencer. Who would tell the memories and stories about Spencer? Would he be forgotten? I realize *now* that Ellen had to move, in order to be the mother she needed to be, and have the support of her parents. As much as she loved Hilton Head, there were too many memories there of Spencer.

On January 22, 2008, John suffered a debilitating stroke, one that left him a prisoner in his own body. He had become paralyzed on his right side, couldn't even smile completely, couldn't talk, and couldn't swallow. His mind was still there, and his eyes and left hand spoke for him. He was always glad to see us, would raise his left hand, and loved company. Many friends came to visit, which meant so much to him and to us. I try to visit the sick often now, but never enough, I'm afraid.

Also, the housing market was getting worse every minute. People looked at our house and the river house but didn't buy. We rented the river house and the historic house, too, but with so much money going out for medical bills and the upkeep and repair of the houses, we were in deep trouble.

Medical bills were horrendous. Medicare helps, but when that is gone it is catastrophic. Close Beaufort friends realized how desperate we were. They called me wanting to establish a John Gettys Smith Fund at the bank. I was so grateful, but I told them I never wanted to know how much anyone contributed. I just wanted to know their names and addresses to thank them. The bank agreed, and these friends spread the word all over Beaufort and Hilton Head of our needs. Several friends, who were former coworkers of John's at Sea Pines, wrote letters to previous employees of the Sea Pines Company. Many of those, who had not seen John in twenty or thirty years, sent contributions. The Hilton Head community and all of the Low Country reached out to us, and all who gave saved us from bankruptcy and the loss of both houses. We weren't able to sell either home quickly, and this fund kept us afloat. There are no words to express my thanks for the compassion shown to my family. I feel so blessed and humbled to have lived in such supportive communities, surrounded by such kind, giving, and true friends.

Epilogue

So many friends keep asking which stories are in this book. One new Hilton Head friend recently asked, "Nelle, when did you move to the Island?" When I replied, "1963", she gasped. "Wow! Then you know where all the bodies are buried." And she's probably right, I do!

Others ask, "Oh, I know, Nelle, you'll tell about the time we did ... this or that?" Surely, I could tell the rat story, the first Christmas tree lighting on Sea Pines Circle, the July Fourth parties on the beach with the papier mâché statues, and many more favorite ones! Sometimes I answer, "Oh, you're right! I should tell that one." Often, you will think differently about some of my stories and *my* recall of the incidents. You may think, "No, Nelle, that wasn't the way it was." That's because they are *your* memories of the story instead of mine, which are just as good. Be proud of them. There is so much more to tell that I don't want to stop yet. But I must. Or we'll just have to write another book.

During the late '70s, '80s, '90s, and on, many wonderful and sad times happened. Many friends came in and out of our lives. Our beloved Sea Pines survived in bad economic times, which has been well documented with the Heritage Foundation, Joe Fraser, Simon Fraser, John Curry, Angus Cotton, the Honorable Sol Blatt, and many others. The Heritage has survived under the excellence of Steve Wilmot and his staff. Many Sea Pines executives moved and began their own new beautiful communities using much of the template of planning of Sea Pines. Some moved to nearby Bluffton. Some moved to greener pastures elsewhere. Many have moved to be near their grown children. Many have moved to a quieter place, as the Island used to be.

However, wonderful people still live here, and many more will continue to move here as long as we protect the beauty and contribute to our churches and our community.

I feel so blessed to have been able to share my memories of the early years of Hilton Head. I have had such a treasured life, and I am so fortunate to have lived there for thirty-three years and been a part of this Paradise. As my father often said, "Always be very proud of where you live, and live so that the place will be proud of you."

I would like to close with a beautiful paragraph that John wrote about Hilton Head in 1963, many, many years ago. I hope it will inspire you to take care of this special place, our Hilton Head Island. Be vigilant and stand up for it.

The Island

Written by John Gettys Smith, 1963

The Island lies like a great green giant just off the vibrant marshes and bluffs of the lower coast of South Carolina. Only a few short years ago, Hilton Head Island was known only to residents of this corner of Carolina and to a handful of hunters who belonged to a gun club and came down from the hills to kill game on the semitropical Island. There was no bridge. There was not even a ferry in those days. The land and its people, almost exclusively the descendants of slaves from a palmy plantation past, seemed caught up in an evergreen time capsule. This capsule was opened in 1956 when the bridge and causeways, named for South Carolina's eminent statesman, James F. Byrnes, linked Hilton Head via Pinckney Island to the mainland. It was more than just a concrete and steel link. It bridged nearly a century of the Island's somnolence. Over this span newcomers brought bright ideas, dreams and a little money toward making those luminous concepts come true. Behind them came a tiny trickle of visitors to this honest Eden. Then came simple accommodations and fare for those who sought such a place. Once here, some could not bear to leave, and seaside homes of contemporary style and simplicity were erected within the trees and behind the dunes. The beach was virgin and so were the forests, and those who came to Hilton Head came to fit into this format, not to dominate it. They were all people with dreams, and they felt they had found them in the reality of sunny days and crystal clear nights when the billions of stars twinkled unmarked by the interfering lights of man's intrusion.

John Gettys Smith on the beach at Sea Pines Plantation in the early days.

POSTCARD BY PHOTO ART

Hilton Head Island Timeline

With Our Memories

1949

A group of lumber associates (General Joseph B. Fraser, Fred C. Hack, Olin T. McIntosh, and C. C. Stebbins) bought a total of twenty thousand acres of pine forest on Hilton Head's southern end for an average of nearly sixty dollars an acre.

1950

The first electricity was brought to the Island by Palmetto Electric Cooperative.

1952

Wilton Graves opened the SeaCrest Motel on Forest Beach. At first, it consisted of two rooms. The first vacation cottages were developed on Folly Field Road.

1955

Roadside Rest, the first restaurant, opened on October 9 with Mrs. J. T. McElveen as the owner.

1956

The James Byrnes Bridge, a two-lane toll bridge, opened July 7. This was the first bridge connecting Hilton Head to the mainland. The toll was $2.50 per round trip.

Charles E. Fraser bought his father's land and began Sea Pines.

The Richardsons moved to Hilton Head and opened the first supermarket on the Island near Coligny Circle. The Richardsons—Norris and Lois, and children Mary Catherine, "J.R.," and Collins—came here along with Lois's mother, Mrs. Herring. When we moved to the Island, Mrs. Herring often babysat for our children. She was like a grandmother to them—she read stories, played games, and especially liked to put together puzzles.

The Hilton Head Island Chamber of Commerce was established.

1957

The first lot in Sea Pines Plantation was sold to Mrs. Reuben Clark of Savannah.

Honey Horn Chapel began Presbyterian services.

1958

Beachfront lots initially sold for $5,350.

1959

The William Hilton Inn, a fifty-six-room hotel on the present-day site of Marriott's Grand Ocean Resort, opened its doors on July 3, beginning formally the opening of Sea Pines residential development. The Inn was designed by Mr. Richard (Pete) McGinty and his associates.

In May, Peggy and Jim Dunbar, along with their children, Dottie and Stewart, opened the Palmetto Bay Marina.

1960

Designed by George Cobb, the Ocean Course in Sea Pines became the first golf course built on Hilton Head Island.

On August 6, Hargray Telephone Company brought telephone service to the Island with a total of 161 business and residential customers.

Walter Greer, our first resident artist, moved to the Island and lived in Sea Pines.

The McIntosh family subdivided 360 acres of the Hilton Head Company to start Spanish Wells.

Port Royal Plantation was developed by Hilton Head Company, led by Fred Hack.

The Island Shop was opened in February by Charles and Sallie Doughtie.

In September, John and Nelle, Gettys (six), Spencer (four), and Ora Elliott (two) moved to Hilton Head. We were listed in the "News Lines from Sea Pines." We lived in the Cordillo Apartments #8.

Jim Van Landingham directed the William Hilton Inn's first children's program for the summer season and through the fall. He did a most credible "one-man job" of looking after the children, and they adored him! They nicknamed him "Mr. V."

In June, the Adventure Inn (named for William Hilton's boat) was opened as a forty-four-room deluxe motel by the Atlantic Development Company. The head of this company was Mr. G. H. McBride, the father of Nancy Gebhardt (Mrs. Carl Gebhardt).

Charles and Mary Fraser got married on November 30 in a grand affair.

St. Luke's Episcopal Church had its first Tour of Homes to raise money for its Building Fund, which needed sixty thousand dollars more, as thirty-four thousand dollars had already been raised. Tickets were five dollars, and the William Hilton Inn and Adventure

Inn offered tour luncheon meals for two dollars each, tax included. What a great price that was!

1964

Charles sent our family to three resorts with well-respected children's programs to gather ideas for our program.

Donald O'Quinn started out being "In Charge of the Turf" on our only eighteen-hole Ocean Course. The course operated then on an annual budget of sixty-five thousand dollars. Don grew up in the area, and Charles hired him early for his help. He became an indispensable part of the growth of the golf courses and land development.

Wallace (Wally) Palmer, a PGA professional, operated the Pro Shop with the help of Clyde Boyd.

The famous Captain's Table restaurant opened at the SeaCrest Motel. It was our first gourmet restaurant.

Sea Pines and the William Hilton Inn were featured on TV, narrated by John in a half-hour video. Very exciting!

Groundbreaking of St. Luke's was held. I can name every person in the photo.

Dr. Chet Goddard, our first doctor, moved to the Island to practice at the Sea Pines Medical Center, which was under construction.

1965

The Sea Pines Medical Center, which served the entire Island, was built on land donated by Charles Fraser. I believe the current CVS, or another pharmacy on Pope Avenue, is the original site of the Medical Center. Mrs. Edith Boyd was the nurse in charge.

The Harold Depkins and the Frank Schaefers and their children moved to the Island. They began planning and contracting for a complex of apartments or condominiums on a six-acre site adjoining the tenth fairway of the Ocean Course. Because the demand was so great, the forty-three villas were sold out before they were built. (Wish we could have bought one.)

We moved into our new house in July, at 48 Beach Lagoon, Sea Pines. The numbers were changed later on to 9 Beach Lagoon. The first mailboxes were painted a forest green with names in gold and black. A small wooden sign with the last name of the home owner was placed nearby, usually nailed to a tree. I still have ours.

Jointly owned by the Sea Pines Company and the Forest Beach Service District, the fire station, with a fire engine that cost $17,500, opened on Cordillo Road. It served all of the south end of the Island at that time.

The first house was built in Port Royal Plantation.

Doug Corkern and Ed Wiggins designed the three-hundred-thousand-dollar Sea Pines Plantation Golf House.

The First Presbyterian Church began services in its new Fellowship Hall, designed by architect Pete McGinty, on March 21. It was used as a temporary sanctuary until the permanent sanctuary was built. According to a quote from the Hilton Head Chamber of Commerce, "The Fellowship Hall includes a classroom wing for Sunday School, rough sawn wide cypress planks create a striking interior for the hall, and the brick exterior walls blend well into the tree-lined site."

The earliest shops that opened adjacent to the William Hilton Inn were Harrison Payne, specializing in sportswear and owned by Don Jones and Jay McDonald; the Vagabond Shop, specializing in antiques and decorative accessories and owned by Mr. and Mrs. Horace Durston; and Wingfields, which also specialized in ladies and men's sportswear, owned by Mr. and Mrs. Wingfield Short. The Shorts had a little girl, Melanie, who was a welcome addition to the few young girls on the Island.

The Chamber of Commerce received complaints on the overemphasis on growth and lot sales. (Imagine that happening then.) The letters point out that the writers chose Hilton Head as a place to get away from the hustle and bustle, and they are somewhat alarmed by all the "boom" writings in the Newsletter! (April 14, 1965)

The *Island Bulletin* was our first printed communication for Islanders, kind of like a newspaper. It was produced weekly with the help of volunteers, headed by Mrs. Helen Brooks, and the Chamber of Commerce. The subscription rate was $3.50 per year, and we all enjoyed receiving our mimeographed copies of happenings on the Island.

The early advertising ads in the *Wall Street Journal* were so innovative. The first one read, "No Neon." The next ad read, "No Neon Continued." Still another proclaimed, "Our Stop Signs Are Green."

Joseph (Joe) B. Fraser and his wife, Carolyn Bexley (Becky) Fraser, and their young children moved to Hilton Head. He founded Sea Pines Homebuilders and in 1968 he joined his younger brother, Charles, in the Sea Pines Plantation Company. He became a vital part over the next ten years as they developed some of the finest large-scale resort and second-home communities in North America. He is widely credited with being instrumental in keeping the Heritage Golf Tournament on Hilton Head Island and establishing the Heritage Classic Foundation in 1987 as a 501(c)(3) nonprofit organization.

1966

The Sea Pines Plantation Club opened in May. Before opening, it had tasting parties and participants voted on dishes.

Mr. and Mrs. Charles Bates (Charlie and Jean) moved with their eight children to Hilton Head. Charles was one of the early talented architects, beginning with the Greenwood Development Company in Palmetto Dunes. The family dramatically doubled our St. Luke's

Sunday School. (I was so afraid they would be Baptists or Presbyterians, as there were no other churches on the Island then!)

Planter's Hall, an addition to the William Hilton Inn, was opened in August, providing space for small and large conventions, a dance floor, and stage.

These additions made it possible to have native South Carolinians who were in Who's Who to be royally entertained during their stay. The South Carolina Homecoming took place November 18–22, one of John's great marketing ideas. Sea Pines sold so much property after that event.

Dr. Bill Fries joined Dr. Chet Goddard on September 6, already expanding the practice.

Dr. Joseph List, our first dentist, moved to the Island in June.

Sea Pines Academy, which later became Hilton Head Prep, opened in September with a total of twenty-nine children. John was put in charge with the help of Harold Depkin and Tommy Wamsley. Nancy Gebhardt was also a strong promoter of the Academy.

The first horseback riding instruction for children opened as Baynard Fields Farm by Mrs. Jarvis Depkin, assisted by Mrs. Nancy Butler. They began their program with only five ponies.

Bruce Devlin represented Sea Pines as a Touring Golf Professional.

Construction on Interstate 95 began, with a target date of completion in 1967 or 1968.

Dennie and Fran McCrary and their children moved to the Island, and he became the vice president of finance for the Sea Pines Company. Several years later, he accepted the position of president and chief operating officer of the Sea Island Company.

Gordon and Genie Craighead and their three daughters moved to the Island. Gordon became the general manager of the William Hilton Inn.

Mr. Eddie Carter was promoted to vice president and construction coordinator of Sea Pines Homebuilders.

The first annual Sea Pines Academy Fashion Show and Dance was held on December 1.

Jim Palmer, our second talented resident artist, and his wife Barbara moved to the Island and made it their home.

1967

On March 22, Arnold Palmer "Saves the Day for Bruce Devlin," so the headlines read.

Mr. Bill Carson was put in charge of maintenance of the Ocean Course and the Sea Marsh Course, which was under construction.

The first Marsh Tacky Race took place on Thursday, October 19. John saved the original mimeographed copy of the first races, which were held on the beach, as I remember.

Sea Pines Plantation installed the Island's first gate with a full-time security guard and began collecting a one-dollar fee for guests. Golfers could deduct this payment from their green fees. There were no shops at that time within Harbour Town or Sea Pines Center.

The Palmetto Dunes area was acquired from the Hilton Head Agricultural Company by Palmetto Dunes Corporation, headed by William T. Gregory, for one thousand dollars per acre.

Construction began on the Harbour Town's red-and-white-striped Lighthouse. It was not completed until 1970.

Hudson's has been a family-owned business since the 1920s, owned and named by Mr. J. B. Hudson Sr. It was primarily a seafood processing plant, specializing in oysters. He and his family began serving meals of shrimp and fish in the dining room, and in 1967 the operation grew to ninety-five seats. I can't remember not going to Hudson's with our little ones, especially when company came to visit us. In 1975, Gloria and Brian Carmines purchased Hudson's, and a new family tradition began. The family immediately became active in the community, and Hudson's became the most coveted place to work for a summer job. Their son, Andrew, is in charge now, and it is still the most popular fresh seafood restaurant—it is simply the best.

1968

The "Big Snow" fell for the first time in twenty years on February 8.

Todd Ballantine, a naturalist and author of *Tideland Treasures*, moved to the Island.

Harbour Town Golf Links, designed by Pete Dye and Jack Nicklaus, began preparations for the Harbour Town Course.

Mary Wyman Stone Fraser founded Sea Pines Montessori School, the first Montessori school in South Carolina. Sally Cook was the directress, with her daughter, Jennifer, as helper. Class was held in one room of the Tree House Restaurant complex, now a convenience store on South Forest Beach.

Mr. James (Jim) Light came to work for Charles after graduating from Harvard Business School. He became executive vice president of community development and then, ultimately, the chief operating officer.

The first fast-food restaurant, called the Fin 'N Feather, was owned by Eddie Howell. The Kuechlers bought it in the early 1970s.

1969–1973

This era was known by many as the Boom Years.

1969

Mr. James (Jim) Chaffin first met Charles and joined the Sea Pines Company, working in many areas. Charles often hired talented people and advised them to "Go fill a vacuum." Jim became the senior vice president of marketing in 1974.

The first Heritage Golf Tournament took place November 27–30, the Thanksgiving weekend. Our lives were changed forever. Arnie Palmer winning this tournament, after not having won a tournament for fourteen months, was an enormous happening. The stories and television coverage were music to everyone's ears.

The first library in a trailer was dedicated by Mr. Jonathan Daniels in mid-February.

1970

The *Island Packet* was first published on July 9.

The Hilton Head Company started Shipyard Plantation.

The Quarterdeck Bar in Harbour Town opened. It quickly became a meeting place for all the locals and is now a favorite of tourists, too.

1971

Stan Smith became the first Sea Pines Tennis Touring Pro in May and played that summer at Wimbledon.

Mr. E. T. (Tommy) Baysden began his marketing career with the Sea Pines Public Relations Department. He worked at many fine resorts afterward and retired after being at Palmetto Bluff.

On August 6, Nell's Harbour Shop opened, first called the Hilton Head Harbour Shop. I omitted the "e" on Nell's because I didn't want the shop called "Nellies."

The Tennis Tournament of Champions was held August 27–29 at the Harbour Town Racquet Club at Sea Pines. It is often called the WCT (World Championship Tennis, Inc.). John was the first chairman, and I still have the program.

Sea Pines acquired land on the north end of the Island, which was developed into Hilton Head Plantation.

The first Annual Sea Pines Billfishing Tournament was held. By

1973, fifty-two boats competed for the ten-thousand-dollar event, and sixteen blue marlins were caught in a most successful tournament. I remember meeting so many people from the Low Country and Beaufort, especially Summer Pingree and Tom Garrett, who both won some of the tournaments.

1972

After renaming the event for brevity, the First Annual CBS Tennis Classic was held at Sea Pines Racquet Club in Harbour Town, March 21–24.

The Island Theater in Coligny Plaza was opened by Mr. Paul Ramsey.

It's amazing how much talent—in every field—moved to this Island in the '60s and early '70s. I feel many artists and illustrators arrived here because they were captivated by the Island's beauty. The Bowlers (Joe and Marilyn Bowler, with their daughters, Jolyn and Brynne) moved to Sea Pines. Coby and Virginia Whitmore, with their son Tom, had already moved here and they were good friends. Coby had urged the Bowlers to move here, too. Another illustrator friend, Joe DeMers, had not only moved to the Island but had started an art gallery at Harbour Town, a few doors from Nell's.

Stan Smith won Wimbledon over Ilie Nastase in a five-setter and by the year's end was the world's number-one singles player. His style of tennis shoe, white leather with green trim, quickly became the most successful selling sneaker for the Adidas Company, still selling millions today. "Most people think I'm a shoe!" says a humble Stan Smith.

1973

The Sea Pines University Tour of Resorts, across the United States on two chartered planes, was enjoyed by 169 people, January 7–14. It was an unbelievable experience!

The Second Annual CBS Tennis Classic was held at Sea Pines, March 11–18.

The first Family Circle Tennis Tournament was held April 30–May 6 at Sea Pines Plantation and was aired on NBC.

Ed Pinckney, one of the early Island landscape architects, was urged by Charles Fraser to move here with his wife, Johnnie, and their six children. He had won many architectural awards. He always stressed Charles Fraser's feeling that houses in Sea Pines should be landscape blending, to allow a small, inexpensive home to be next door to a very expensive one. There were no white houses then.

In March, the Hofbrauhaus Restaurant opened on Pope Avenue and was an instant success, our first German culinary experience.

Berry and Ruthie Edwards opened the Greenery Inc. on Highway 278. They quickly made friends and became a part of every organization. They have been outstanding Islanders, contributing much to the community and especially to the arts.

John Gettys Smith resigned from Sea Pines Company on December 20 and formed his own public relations firm: John Gettys Smith Associates.

1974

The Heritage was first televised.

The Hilton Head Island swing bridge was struck by a barge, which stopped all traffic across the bridge for six weeks. As I remember, the pontoon bridge took two weeks to construct, and another four weeks passed before traffic flowed across the swing bridge.

1975

The Hilton Head Hospital was completed. We were so excited to have it! The hospital was among the early clients of John's PR firm, John Gettys Smith Associates.

Mrs. Dorothy Olbert, age fifty, was murdered. It was the first such heinous crime on the Island that I remember. Though it's still unsolved, old-time Islanders think they know who did it.

1979

Hurricane David missed the Island, thankfully, but high winds left beaches eroded and destroyed several Singleton Beach homes.

1982

Wexford Plantation and Long Cove Club were developed.

The Seabrook, the first retirement community on Hilton Head, opened its doors in October.

1983

The Town of Hilton Head Island incorporated as a municipality. This was a godsend for the town to have restrictions on the environment not in a plantation. Eventually, greed by some would harm the Island's beauty. The town's first offices were housed in the John Gettys Smith Building, formerly the original Bargain Box.

Charles Fraser stepped down as chairman of the Sea Pines Company.

1986

Our bronze alligator disappeared from in front of the Plantation Club and showed up at Luke Taylor's home in Palm Beach.

At a Halloween party that year, John and I went as Mr. and Mrs. Luke Taylor with huge alligator "blown-up floats" hanging around our necks. We won first prize!

1987

Nelle opened a second shop called Nell's at Wexford with Ora Smith as the manager.

1991

The original treehouse in our first playground was torn down to make way for the Sea Pines Racquet Club's new tennis station. The children loved the split-level treehouse, which had many inscriptions carved into the beams, like "Hayden loves Jenny." I remember Mary Fraser had a big role in planning of this playground, to be made of wood and all-natural materials, with no plastic or artificial materials.

The treehouse had served the Island well for twenty-one years, and old-timers hated to see it go. Change is difficult, but the playground and facility at Harbour Town are exactly what Sea Pines needs now.

1992

John wrote a letter to secure funds to erect a statue in honor of Charles Fraser on September 14. At that time, Charles was suffering financially and physically undergoing lymphoma treatment, and nothing had been done to honor him yet.

1996

Spencer and Ellen Churchill were married in St. Luke's Episcopal Church on March 16. The reception was held in the original Plantation Club dining room. It was one of the happiest times in our lives.

We sold Nell's Harbour Shop on March 31.

In September, John and I moved to Beaufort to live and restore an antebellum home at 901 Prince Street.

2002

Charles Fraser, age seventy-three, died in a boating accident in the Turks and Caicos Islands on December 15. What a tragic loss of this genius of a man. His funeral was held at Harbour Town with a huge crowd of mourners. He was buried under the memorial statue that had been dedicated to his life. Such a fitting resting place for him.

2006

On August 24, John and I bought a house on the river in Seabrook. All three of our children were so excited about enjoying this riverside property. Tragically on September 11, Spencer was struck by an aortic aneurysm and died during surgery two days later. It was such paralyzing sorrow to all of us, leaving behind his beloved wife, Ellen, and three young children: Christine, nine; Cotter, five; and Samantha, three.

2008

On January 22, John had his third stroke, a debilitating one this time, which left him paralyzed on his right side. We kept praying that he could respond to treatments to overcome the damage he had suffered. He fought valiantly for over a year.

2009

John passed away on February 24, and at his funeral there was a joyous celebration of his life. At the graveside service, Joe Harden, one of the early Hilton Head homebuilders, said to a friend, "You know, John was probably responsible for my success. Charles Fraser had the idea, but John made it happen. Advertising for heaven will be at an all-time high with John there!"

I love to walk

the beaches here.

There isn't anything

that can bring you down

to size like walking a beach

and looking at the majesty

of God's handiwork.

CHARLOTTE JONES,

former Hilton Head kindergarten teacher